15 Days of Prayer
With Saint Elizabeth Ann Seton

Also in the *15 Days of Prayer* collection:

Saint Teresa of Ávila

The Curé of Ars

Pierre Teilhard de Chardin

Saint Bernard

Saint Augustine

Meister Eckhart

Thomas Merton

Saint Louis de Montfort

Saint Benedict

Charles de Foucauld

Saint Francis de Sales

Johannes Tauler

Saint Dominic

Don Bosco

Saint Alphonsus Liguori

Saint John of the Cross

Saint Thérèse of Lisieux

Saint Catherine of Siena

Saint Bernadette of Lourdes

Saint Thomas Aquinas

Saint Faustina Kowalska

15 DAYS OF PRAYER
WITH
Saint
Elizabeth Ann Seton

BETTY ANN McNEIL, D.C.

Liguori
LIGUORI, MISSOURI

Published by Liguori Publications
Liguori, Missouri
http://www.liguori.org
http://www.catholicbooksonline.com

Imprimi Potest:
Richard Thibodeau, C.Ss.R.
Provincial, Denver Province
The Redemptorists

Copyright 2002 by Betty Ann McNeil

Library of Congress Cataloging-in-Publication Data

McNeil, Betty Ann
    15 days of prayer with Saint Elizabeth Ann Seton / Betty Ann McNeil.
        p. cm.
    Includes bibliographical references.
    ISBN 0-7648-0841-9 (pbk.)
    1. Seton, Elizabeth Ann, Saint, 1774–1821—Meditations. 2. Spiritual life—Catholic Church. I. Title: Fifteen days of prayer with Saint Elizabeth Ann Seton. II. Title.

BX4700.S4 M36 2002
269'.6—dc21   2002016116

Printed in the United States of America
06 05 04 03 02   5 4 3 2 1
First edition

Table of Contents

Acknowledgments

THE WRITER AND READERS owe a debt of gratitude to all who have preserved the original writings of Elizabeth Bayley Seton. The prototypical archivist of the Seton papers, Reverend Simon Gabriel Bruté, first recognized their value and safeguarded them, advising others to do likewise in the future. Many of the Seton writings in this work are used courtesy of the Archives Saint Joseph's Provincial House, Daughters of Charity, Emmitsburg, Maryland.

The writer wishes to acknowledge with gratitude the kind permission of archivists to quote Seton documents from the following other collections: Sister Rita King, S.C., Archives Mount Saint Vincent, Sisters of Charity of Saint Vincent de Paul of New York; Sister Genevieve Keusenkothen, D.C., Archives Marillac Provincial House, Daughters of Charity, Saint Louis, Missouri; Sister Judith Metz, S.C., Archives Mount Saint Joseph, Sisters of Charity of Cincinnati, Ohio; Dr. Wendy Clauson Schlereth, University of Notre Dame Archives, Notre Dame, Indiana; Sister Mary Catherine Seli, S.C., Archives Sisters of Charity of Seton Hill, Greensburg, Pennsylvania; and Reverend Paul K. Thomas, Archives Archdiocese of Baltimore. All excerpts of Seton documents are used with permission. No part of them may be reproduced by any means without permission in writing from the copyright owners. All rights reserved.

With gratitude to the following authors, editors, and copyright owners for permission to cite and quote from the following publications: Regina Bechtle, S.C., and Judith Metz, S.C., Ellin

M. Kelly, mss. ed., *Elizabeth Bayley Seton Collected Writings* (New City Press: New York, 2000); Ellin M. Kelly, Ph.D., and Annabelle M. Melville, eds., *Elizabeth Seton Selected Writings* (Paulist Press: Mahwah, New Jersey, 1987); Sister Catherine Madigan, D.C., for Ellin M. Kelly, Ph.D., *Numerous Choirs. A Chronicle of Elizabeth Bayley Seton and Her Spiritual Daughters. Volume I. The Seton Years: 1774–1821* (Daughters of Charity Mater Dei Provincialate: Evansville, Indiana: 1981).

The cover illustration, the Filicchi portrait of Saint Elizabeth Ann Seton, is courtesy of the Archives Saint Joseph's Provincial House, Daughters of Charity, Emmitsburg, Maryland. On behalf of all beneficiaries of the Seton Legacy, the author wishes to express profound gratitude to Ellin M. Kelly, Ph.D., for her years of dedication to meticulous transcription of the Seton papers and for her scholarship on Elizabeth Bayley Seton. This work benefited from the competent technical and production assistance of Mrs. Selin James and Mrs. Bonnie Weatherly and from the insights and comments of the following readers: Reverend Stephen P. Trzecieski, C.M., Sister Mary Patricia Winters, D.C., Sister Mary Jean Horne, D.C., and Ms. Jeanne Meister. Elizabeth Seton lived her life with an attitude of gratitude and so with "a thankful heart" the writer acknowledges the behind-the-scenes efforts of everyone who contributed to this work in any way.

How to Use This Book

AN OLD CHINESE PROVERB, or at least what I am able to recall of what is supposed to be an old Chinese proverb, goes something like this: "Even a journey of a thousand miles begins with a single step." When you think about it, the truth of the proverb is obvious. It is impossible to begin any project, let alone a journey, without taking the first step. I think it might also be true, although I cannot recall if another Chinese proverb says it, "that the first step is often the hardest." Or, as someone else once observed, "the distance between a thought and the corresponding action needed to implement the idea takes the most energy." I don't know who shared that perception with me but I am certain it was not an old Chinese master!

With this ancient proverbial wisdom, and the not-so-ancient wisdom of an unknown contemporary sage still fresh, we move from proverbs to presumptions. How do these relate to the task before us?

I am presuming that if you are reading this introduction it is because you are contemplating a journey. My presumption is that you are preparing for a spiritual journey and that you have taken at least some of the first steps necessary to prepare for this journey. I also presume, and please excuse me if I am making too many presumptions, that in your preparation for the spiritual journey you have determined that you need a guide. From deep within the recesses of your deepest self, there was something that called you to consider Elizabeth Ann Seton as a potential companion. If my presumptions are correct, may I congratulate you on this decision? I think you have made a wise choice, a choice that can be confirmed by yet another source of wisdom, the wisdom that comes from practical experience.

Even an informal poll of experienced travelers will reveal a common opinion; it is very difficult to travel alone. Some might observe that it is even foolish. Still others may be even stronger in their opinion and go so far as to insist that it is necessary to have a guide, especially when you are traveling into uncharted waters and into territory that you have not yet experienced. I am of the personal opinion that a traveling companion is welcome under all circumstances. The thought of traveling alone, to some exciting destination without someone to share the journey with does not capture my imagination or channel my enthusiasm. However, with that being noted, what is simply a matter of preference on the normal journey becomes a matter of necessity when a person embarks on a spiritual journey.

The spiritual journey, which can be the most challenging of all journeys, is experienced best with a guide, a companion, or at the very least, a friend in whom you have placed your trust. This observation is not a preference or an opinion but rather an established spiritual necessity. All of the great saints with whom I am familiar had a spiritual director or a confessor who journeyed with them. Admittedly, at times the saint might well have traveled far beyond the experience of their guide and companion but more often than not they would return to their director and reflect on their experience. Understood in this sense, the director and companion provided a valuable contribution and necessary resource.

When I was learning how to pray (a necessity for anyone who desires to be a full-time and public "religious person"), the community of men that I belong to gave me a great gift. Between my second and third year in college, I was given a one-year sabbatical, with all expenses paid and all of my personal needs met. This period of time was called novitiate. I was officially designated as a novice, a beginner in the spiritual journey, and I was assigned a "master," a person who was willing to lead me. In addition to the master, I was provided with every imaginable book and any other resource that I could possibly need. Even with all that I was provided, I did not learn how to pray because of the books and the unlimited resources, rather it was the master, the companion who was the key to the experience.

One day, after about three months of reading, of quiet and solitude, and of practicing all of the methods and descriptions of prayer that were available to me, the master called. "Put away the books, forget the method, and just listen." We went into a room, became quiet, and tried to recall the presence of God, and then, the master simply prayed out loud and permitted me to listen to his prayer. As he prayed, he revealed his hopes, his dreams, his struggles, his successes, and most of all, his relationship with God. I discovered as I listened that his prayer was deeply intimate but most of all it was self-revealing. As I learned about him, I was led through his life experience to the place where God dwells. At that moment I was able to understand a little bit about what I was supposed to do if I really wanted to pray.

The dynamic of what happened when the master called, invited me to listen, and then revealed his innermost self to me as he communicated with God in prayer, was important. It wasn't so much that the master was trying to reveal to me what needed to be said; he was not inviting me to pray with the same words that he used, but rather that he was trying to bring me to that place within myself where prayer becomes possible. That place, a place of intimacy and of self-awareness, was a necessary stop on the journey and it was a place that I needed to be led to. I could not have easily discovered it on my own.

The purpose of the volume that you hold in your hand is to lead you, over a period of fifteen days or, maybe more realistically, fifteen prayer periods, to a place where prayer is possible. If you already have a regular experience and practice of prayer, perhaps this volume can help lead you to a deeper place, a more intimate relationship with the Lord.

It is important to note that the purpose of this book is not to lead you to a better relationship with Elizabeth Ann Seton, your spiritual companion. Although your companion will invite you to share some of their deepest and most intimate thoughts, your companion is doing so only to bring you to that place where God dwells. After all, the true measurement of a companion for the journey is that they bring you to the place where you need to be, and then they step back, out of the picture. A guide who brings you to the desired destination and then sticks around is a very unwelcome guest!

Many times I have found myself attracted to a particular idea or method for accomplishing a task, only to discover that what seemed to be inviting and helpful possessed too many details. All of my energy went to the mastery of the details and I soon lost my enthusiasm. In each instance, the book that seemed so promising ended up on my bookshelf, gathering dust. I can assure you, it is not our intention that this book end up in your bookcase, filled with promise, but unable to deliver.

There are three simple rules that need to be followed in order to use this book with a measure of satisfaction.

Place: It is important that you choose a place for reading that provides the necessary atmosphere for reflection and that does not allow for too many distractions. Whatever place you choose needs to be comfortable, have the necessary lighting, and, finally, have a sense of "welcoming" about it. You need to be able to look forward to the experience of the journey. Don't travel steerage if you know you will be more comfortable in first class and if the choice is realistic for you. On the other hand, if first class is a distraction and you feel more comfortable and more yourself in steerage, then it is in steerage that you belong.

My favorite place is an overstuffed and comfortable chair in my bedroom. There is a light over my shoulder, and the chair reclines if I feel a need to recline. Once in a while, I get lucky and the sun comes through my window and bathes the entire room in light. I have other options and other places that are available to me but this is the place that I prefer.

Time: Choose a time during the day when you are most alert and when you are most receptive to reflection, meditation, and prayer. The time that you choose is an essential component. If you are a morning person, for example, you should choose a time that is in the morning. If you are more alert in the afternoon, choose an afternoon time slot; and if evening is your preference, then by all means choose the evening. Try to avoid "peak" periods in your daily routine when you know that you might be disturbed. The time that you choose needs to be your time and needs to work for you.

It is also important that you choose how much time you will spend with your companion each day. For some it will be possible to set aside enough time in order to read and reflect on all the material that is offered for a given day. For others, it might not be possible to devote one time to the suggested material for the day, so the prayer period may need to be extended for two, three, or even more sessions. It is not important how long it takes you; it is only important that it works for you and that you remain committed to that which is possible.

For myself I have found that fifteen minutes in the early morning, while I am still in my robe and pajamas and before my morning coffee, and even before I prepare myself for the day, is the best time. No one expects to see me or to interact with me because I have not yet "announced" the fact that I am awake or even on the move. However, once someone hears me in the bathroom, then my window of opportunity is gone. It is therefore important to me that I use the time that I have identified when it is available to me.

Freedom: It may seem strange to suggest that freedom is the third necessary ingredient, but I have discovered that it is most important. By freedom I understand a certain "stance toward life," a "permission to be myself and to be gentle and understanding of who I am." I am constantly amazed at how the human person so easily sets himself or herself up for disappointment and perceived failure. We so easily make judgments about ourselves and our actions and our choices, and very often those judgments are negative, and not at all helpful.

For instance, what does it really matter if I have chosen a place and a time, and I have missed both the place and the time for three days in a row? What does it matter if I have chosen, in that twilight time before I am completely awake and still a little sleepy, to roll over and to sleep for fifteen minutes more? Does it mean that I am not serious about the journey, that I really don't want to pray, that I am just fooling myself when I say that my prayer time is important to me? Perhaps, but I prefer to believe that it simply means that I am tired and I just wanted a little more sleep. It doesn't mean anything more than that. However, if I make it mean more than that, then I can become discouraged, frustrated, and put myself into a state where I might more easily give up. "What's the use? I might as well forget all about it."

The same sense of freedom applies to the reading and the praying of this text. If I do not find the introduction to each day helpful, I don't need to read it. If I find the questions for reflection at the end of the appointed day repetitive, then I should choose to close the book and go my own way. Even if I discover that the reflection offered for the day is not the one that I prefer and that the one for the next day seems more inviting, then by all means, go on to the one for the next day.

That's it! If you apply these simple rules to your journey you should receive the maximum benefit and you will soon find yourself at your destination. But be prepared to be surprised. If you have never been on a spiritual journey you should know that the "travel brochures" and the other descriptions that you might have heard are nothing compared to the real thing. There is so much more than you can imagine.

REV. THOMAS M. SANTA, CSsR
LIGUORI, MISSOURI
FEAST OF THE PRESENTATION, 1999

A Brief Chronology of the Life of Saint Elizabeth Ann Seton

August 28, 1774: Born in or near New York City to Dr. Richard Bayley (1744–1801) and Catherine Charlton Bayley (d. 1777).

June 16, 1778: Second marriage of Dr. Bayley to Charlotte Amelia Barclay (1759–1805), followed four months later by the death of Catherine (Kitty) Bayley, (b. 1777), younger sister of Elizabeth.

1782: Makes first of several prolonged visits with her sister Mary to their paternal uncle, William LeConte Bayley and his wife Sarah Pell, at their farm in New Rochelle, New York. Lives there for four years and returns to her father's home in 1786 but leaves again in two years to live with relatives until her marriage.

January 25, 1794: Weds William Magee Seton, in the home of Dr. Wright Post and Mary Bayley Post, in lower Manhattan. Later Elizabeth wrote: "My own home at 20—the world—that and heaven too, quite impossible!" (*SW*, 346). William and Elizabeth lived at 27 Wall Street soon after their marriage.

May 3, 1795: Gives birth to a daughter, Anna Maria Seton; William (November 25, 1795); Richard Bayley (July 20, 1798); Catherine Charlton (June 28, 1800); Rebecca Mary (August 20, 1802). All were baptized at Trinity Episcopal Church on Broadway.

November 19, 1803: After sailing to Italy for her husband's health, the Setons are quarantined in the Lazaretto until December 19, then they moved into a rented house at Pisa, Italy, where William Magee Seton, 35, died on December 27 of tuberculosis. He is buried in the English graveyard of Saint John's Anglican Church, Leghorn, Italy. Elizabeth returned to New York in June.

March 14, 1805: Reverend Matthew O'Brien receives Elizabeth's profession of faith to Roman Catholicism at Saint Peter's, Barclay Street. Within two weeks Elizabeth received her first holy Communion on March 25 and was confirmed there on May 25 by Bishop John Carroll (1735–1815), first bishop of Baltimore. Elizabeth took the name of "Mary" as her Confirmation name.

June 9, 1808: The Setons sail on the *Grand Sachem* from New York to Baltimore, Maryland. The travelers arrived June 16, the feast of Corpus Christi, at Saint Mary's Seminary on Paca Street in the midst of the dedication of the new chapel. At this location Elizabeth began a small school for girls.

December 7, 1808: Arrival of Cecilia Marie O'Conway (1788–1865), of Philadelphia, the first candidate and the prototype of the American Sisters of Charity. She may be compared with Marguerite Naseau (1594–1633), of Suresnes, who was the first Daughter of Charity in France.

March 25, 1809: Pronouncement of vows of chastity and obedience for one year before Archbishop John Carroll in the lower chapel at Paca Street. Elizabeth received the title of "Mother Seton."

July 31, 1809: The Sisters of Charity of Saint Joseph's begin living a regular community life in the Stone House, at Emmitsburg, on 269 acres donated by Samuel Sutherland Cooper, a wealthy convert. This date marks the foundation of the first native community of religious women established in the United States.

February 22, 1810: Opening of Saint Joseph's Free School, the first free Catholic school for girls staffed by religious women in the United States. The first pupils were day students from the Emmitsburg area. Saint Joseph's Academy opened May 14 with five boarding pupils from Frederick County, Maryland.

January 17, 1812: Official confirmation of the *Regulations for the Society of the Sisters of Charity in the United States of America*, by Archbishop John Carroll. The American rule is based on the

Common Rules of the Daughters of Charity developed by Vincent de Paul and Louise de Marillac, for the apostolic community they cofounded in Paris, 1633. After completing a novitiate eighteen Sisters of Charity of Saint Joseph's pronounced annual vows for the first time under the modified Vincentian rule on July 19, 1813.

March 12, 1812: Death of Anna Maria (Sister Annina), 16, first vowed member of the Sisters of Charity of Saint Joseph's, and eldest child of Elizabeth Seton, from tuberculosis.

November 3, 1816: Death of Rebecca, 14, youngest child of Elizabeth Seton, from complications of a hip injury after a fall on the ice which resulted in tuberculosis.

September 17, 1818: Completed the first English translation of the earliest biography of Louise de Marillac by Nicolas Gobillon (1676).

January 4, 1821: Death of Elizabeth Seton, 46, in Saint Joseph's House, Emmitsburg, Maryland, and her burial the next day in the original cemetery of the Sisters of Charity in Saint Joseph's Valley. The sacred remains were exhumed in the fall of 1846 and transferred into the vault of the newly completed Mortuary Chapel partially funded by William Seton as a memorial to his mother. The remains were again exhumed October 26, 1962, and now rest in the Basilica of Saint Elizabeth Ann Seton at Emmitsburg, Maryland.

September 14, 1975: Pope Paul VI presided at the canonization and proclaimed that "Elizabeth Ann Bayley Seton is a Saint!" The feast day of Saint Elizabeth Ann Seton, first native-born United States citizen to be canonized by the Roman Catholic Church, is celebrated on January 4. Saint Elizabeth Ann Seton is a pioneer in free Catholic education and may be considered a patron of Catholic schools in the United States.

The *Anima Christi* of Elizabeth Seton:

> *Soul of Jesus, sanctify me.*
> *Blood of Jesus, wash me.*
> *Passion of Jesus, comfort me.*
> *Wounds of Jesus, Hide me.*
> *Heart of Jesus, receive me.*
> *Spirit of Jesus, enliven me.*
> *Goodness of Jesus, pardon me.*
> *Beauty of Jesus, draw me.*
> *Humility of Jesus, humble me.*
> *Peace of Jesus, pacify me.*
> *Love of Jesus, inflame me.*
> *Kingdom of Jesus, come to me.*
> *Grace of Jesus, replenish me.*
> *Mercy of Jesus, pity me.*
> *Sanctity of Jesus, sanctify me.*
> *Purity of Jesus, purify me.*
> *Cross of Jesus, support me.*
> *Nails of Jesus, hold me.*
> *Mouth of Jesus, bless me.*

> *In life, in death—in time and Eternity—*
> *in the hour of Death defend Me.*
> *Call me to come to thee,*
> *receive me with thy Saints in glory everlasting.*

ELIZABETH ANN SETON (*SW*, 337),
ADAPTED FROM A PRAYER OF SAINT IGNATIUS OF LOYOLA (1491–1556)

Abbreviations Used in This Book

ASJPH   Archives, Saint Joseph's Provincial House, Daughters of Charity, Emmitsburg, Maryland

AMSV   Archives, Sisters of Charity of Saint Vincent de Paul of New York

AMSJ   Archives, Sisters of Charity of Cincinnati, Ohio

ASCSH   Archives, Sisters of Charity of Seton Hill, Greensburg, Pennsylvania

UNDA   University of Notre Dame Archives, Notre Dame, Indiana

AG   *Ad Gentes* (Decree on the Church's Missionary Activity)

CC   Meditation on the Communion of the Cross

CPR   Meditation on Communion: Preparation, Reception, Thanks, Eternity

DD   Meditation on Death in Desire

Diary   Leghorn Journal and Diary of 1803–1804

DR   Dear Remembrances

EBS   Elizabeth Bayley Seton Collected Writings

EPG   On the Exercise of the Presence of God

FCI   First Communion Instructions

IDL   Introduction to the Devout Life

IWG   Instruction on the Word of God

LG   *Lumen Gentium* (Dogmatic Constitution on the Church)

Life   The Life of Mrs. Eliza A. Seton

MA   Mother's Advices to Her Daughter, Catherine Josephine Seton

NC   *Numerous Choirs: A Chronicle of Elizabeth Bayley Seton and Her Spiritual Daughters*

Ps   Psalm

SRP   Meditation on Still Reading His Prophet and Seeking for Our Only Joy

SW   Elizabeth Seton Selected Writings

SV   Meditation on Saint Vincent's Day

Introduction

THE PROMINENCE OF ELIZABETH BAYLEY SETON has long been recognized and her contributions to Church and society lauded. "A great woman is a public legacy and should be enjoyed by all ages and in many guises," according to Annabelle McConnell Melville, the definitive Seton biographer, who considered Elizabeth as one of the great women of America. This native of New York and petite wife of William Magee Seton (1768–1803), gave birth to five children within seven years but the happiness, dreams, and hopes of the Setons' marriage were soon shattered by family problems, disease, illness, and financial worries. Elizabeth was faithful to her ill husband and at his death remained adamantly committed to her primary obligations as mother to her "darlings," then ages one to eight.

God led her along a thorny path of poverty, sorrow, and loss. With her deep spirit of faith, she wrote: "If we did not *now know* and love God—if we did not *feel* the consolations, and *embrace* the cheering Hope he has set before us, and *find* our *delight* in the study of his blessed word and truth, what would become of us?" (*SW*, 133). Elizabeth is a valiant woman of faith.

SETON SPIRITUALITY
Elizabeth Bayley Seton was a person whose religious formation was marked by many companions on the journey who enabled her to come to know her God intimately. The Divine One gifted Elizabeth with a steadfast love and confiding hope in the midst of

joys and sorrows. Her spiritual growth was a source of consolation as she lived an ordinary life in an extraordinary manner. She was deeply involved in a personal relationship with her loving Creator. The Word of God and the Eucharist nourished Elizabeth's soul and were the sources which enabled her

- to love her God, her husband, her children, her friends, her pupils, her spiritual advisors, her companions, poor persons, and all of creation;
- to care for orphans, widows, families, and persons living in poverty, by doing works of charity, mercy, and justice;
- to address the unmet needs among poor persons, especially children who lacked schooling and religious education in the faith;
- to commune with nature and walk humbly with her God in prayer, Scripture, worship, and the ways of the Spirit.

Reverend Simon Gabriel Bruté, Elizabeth's spiritual director, had almost daily contact with her for the last ten years of her life. He recorded his impressions of her sanctity after her death and indicated his conviction that "hers was one of those elite souls, with the like characteristics found in Saint Teresa [of Ávila] and Saint Jane Frances de Chantal" (MS, 299). He believed her just as capable of sanctity as they. He also was impressed with her "purity and love of God, heaven, supernatural, and eternal things" (MS, 299).

Elizabeth achieved sainthood not because she converted to Roman Catholicism but because of how she listened and responded to God's will throughout her earthly life. Her holiness developed from her Episcopalian roots set by the patterns of the liturgical life of the Anglican Communion in the Protestant Episcopal Church of New York.

The young Elizabeth overcame her early fears of a judgmental God and as her life of faith matured, she grew into a deeply personal relationship with her gracious God whom she came to know as a God of love. In her memoir *Dear Remembrances*, Elizabeth recalled her lifelong consolation from Psalm 23, which was one of the first prayers she learned as a young child. This psalm was a treasury of grace and always a source of consolation for her. "Though I walk in the midst of the Shadow of Death, I will fear no evil, for thou art with me" (*SW*, 345; see also Ps 23:4).

Like all persons, Elizabeth's path to holiness developed through the way she fulfilled her roles in life as a daughter, wife, mother, social minister, widow, convert, sole parent, educator, Sister of Charity, and saintly foundress. The kaleidoscope of her life emanates from her primary friendship with God. Her myriad associations marked Elizabeth's unique path of sanctification. God's plan for her salvation unfolded through a variety of persons and events, some pivotal and life-changing, which engaged Elizabeth in response and commitment. Her faith-filled way to God provides us with a timeless model of virtuous living.

Elizabeth's spirituality reflects a mosaic of dominant themes which permeated her life and writings. Central to these are her hunger for the Word of God and the Eucharist, her pursuit of the will of God, reliance on Divine Providence, acceptance of the cross of Christ in suffering, service of Jesus Christ in persons who are poor, loyalty to the Church, and her confidence in Mary, the Mother of God. Elizabeth lived her life on *terra firma* but riveted her vision on eternal life. She had a lifelong focus on the promise of salvation and eternal union with God. During her earthly life she also enjoyed the majestic beauty of creation.

Hunger for the Word of God. The Bible was Elizabeth's constant companion throughout her life. She prayed her way through life's joys and struggles with a scriptural accent that revealed her own relationship to God and motivated others in the sacred ways of the Spirit. Being rooted in the Word enabled Elizabeth to accept life serenely on God's terms. She sought to be attentive to God's presence within and around her, praising and loving the Divine in dreary days of darkness as in times of brilliant sunshine.

Thirst for the Eucharist. As an Episcopalian, Elizabeth was a devout communicant and as a Roman Catholic, her belief in the Real Presence of Jesus in the Eucharist sustained her in the mission of charitable service which she undertook along with the Sisters of Charity. Her eucharistic devotion and faith in God's abiding presence nourished her imitation of Jesus Christ as the source and model of all charity. The eucharistic themes of the prayer *The Anima Christi* were dear to Elizabeth's heart.

Pursuit of the Will of God. Pursuing the will of God was the most important continuous thread of Elizabeth's life. She held deep convictions about its centrality, and this formed the core of her spirituality. She had an abiding respect for the mysterious ways of the Almighty. As Elizabeth's knowledge of the Divine intensified, so did her ability to love and serve God in her neighbor.

Reliance on Divine Providence. Elizabeth relied on God despite trials and misfortunes. She entrusted her needs to a most gracious Providence, which never failed her. In a letter to her son William, Elizabeth expressed her belief to him that "our good God has his times and moments for every thing" (November 20, 1814). Achievement and success were not her goal even when she anticipated gainful employment in her attempts to earn a living. "If it succeeds I bless God, if [it] does not succeed...I bless God, because then it will be right that it should not succeed" (*CW*, 362).

Acceptance of the Cross of Christ. Living the Paschal Mystery, the suffering, death, and resurrection of Christ in her own life became very personal for Elizabeth, especially when she faced widowhood in a foreign land at age twenty-nine. The crucible of the Setons' quarantine in the lazaretto enabled her to embrace the cross of Christ more fully in its varied forms of poverty, illness, loss, and injustice. Such experiences comprised the unique stepping stones for her sanctity.

Service of Jesus Christ to Persons Who Are Poor. Serving her neighbor in need was important to Elizabeth throughout her life. She and other devout parishioners of Trinity Episcopal Church in New York founded the Society for the Relief of Poor Widows with Young Children (1797), the first charitable organization managed by women in the United States. This organization assisted impoverished families in crisis. Later in collaboration with French refugee priests belonging to the Society of Saint Sulpice, Elizabeth founded the Sisters of Charity of Saint Joseph's at Emmitsburg, Maryland, in 1809. The mission of her community was to provide charitable service to poor persons in need and to educate young women.

Loyalty to the Church. Having long been devoted to liturgical worship, the dogma of the Eucharistic Presence of Jesus prompted Elizabeth's search for the truths of faith in Roman Catholicism. She actively sought the Church of apostolic succession and prayed to be in the Church of the true faith if she wasn't already. Faith was a gift which God planted deep within Elizabeth's heart. With a grateful heart she considered her decision to enter the Catholic Church to be among the greatest graces of her life. At the end of her life Elizabeth admonished those gathered about her: "Be children of the Church, be children of the Church" (NC, 234).

Confidence in Mary As the Mother of God. Elizabeth identified with the maternity of Mary as the Mother of Jesus, especially in the sufferings she endured at the time of the passion and death of Jesus. Elizabeth also appreciated the intercessory role of Mary in the Church as the mediatrix of the graces of her divine son. *The Memorare* stimulated her spiritual growth and held a special place in Elizabeth's treasury of favorite prayers and devotions.

Promise of Eternity. From Elizabeth's earliest years, despite all the sorrows and crosses of her life, she viewed herself not only as a pilgrim en route through this life, but also as one who faced each day looking forward to God's promise of eternity. The very thought of eternity made her soul dance with anticipation and excited her whole being.

Beauties of Creation. Elizabeth and her sister Mary spent many happy summers at the home of William LeConte Bayley, their paternal uncle, by the Long Island Sound in New Rochelle, New York. Along its seashore Elizabeth first discovered the fragility and beauty of nature in seashells, birds, and flowers. Elizabeth encountered God amid the created beauty of her natural environment, particularly at the seashore or by the mountains.

It was during the Holy Year of 1975 and the International Year of the Woman that a tiny widow from New York and a citizen of the world was proclaimed a saint. As a devout convert, who was also a poet, musician, linguist, mystic, and woman for all seasons, Saint Elizabeth Ann Seton, the first native-born citizen of the United States to be canonized, offers a model of Christlike living for all ages. Her life was real, her way realistic for believers who are also called to holiness.

THE MOTHER OF MANY DAUGHTERS

Just months prior to her death, Elizabeth reported to her dear friend and benefactor, Antonio Filicchi, that the grain of mustard seed he had planted by God's hand had taken root in America. It was flourishing in new foundations of the Sisters of Charity beyond Saint Joseph's Valley at Emmitsburg–Mount Saint Mary's College and Seminary, and also in Philadelphia and New York.

The mission of the Sisters of Charity was rooted in the rule Saint Vincent de Paul (1581–1660) and Saint Louise de Marillac (1591–1660) had given to their Daughters of Charity. Modeled after the French community established in Paris (1633), the American Sisters of Charity initially focused on the education and care of poor children directing their efforts to wherever "our Sweet Providence" may call them (October 19, 1820). Indeed Elizabeth's reliance on Providence to lead and provide for the human family has borne much fruit in North America and throughout the world.

The little mustard seed of the Sisters of Charity has expanded over the years. The Holy Spirit has generated new life for the Church from the mysterious dynamics of events, circumstances, and human relationships. From the original foundation of the Sisters of Charity of Saint Joseph's, several other branches developed which trace their roots to the foundation by Elizabeth Seton at the Stone House in Saint Joseph's Valley, July 31, 1809.

Today the Sisters and Daughters of Charity collaborate in serving the people of God through the Sisters of Charity Federation in the Vincentian and Setonian Tradition. Other congregations based on the rule of Vincent de Paul and Louise de Marillac are also members of this federation.

INSPIRATION FOR ALL AGES

The chapter titles and subtitles of *15 Days of Prayer With Saint Elizabeth Ann Seton* are phrases taken directly from Seton writings. Elizabeth communicated her thoughts and feelings in the typical language of the early nineteenth century as a refined and educated woman of her day. At times her expressions may sound quaint to the modern reader. All citations for quotes taken from *Elizabeth Bayley Seton Collected Writings* refer to volume one of this series (New City Press, 2000).

To understand the way Elizabeth expressed herself regarding God, one must keep in mind that she lived in a patriarchal society, so her writings reflect a different historical and social context from that of the reader. To appreciate the depth of her experience one must overlook politically correct nuances of contemporary language regarding gender issues in favor of the essence of Elizabeth's message. To do otherwise risks missing Elizabeth's unique insights conveyed in her own words and mined from the treasury of her spiritual journey. For example, Elizabeth wrote that "God in his continual presence with us is our Father" (*EPG*, 2). Elizabeth had not known her own mother and appears to have been disconnected early from her stepmother. From Elizabeth's personal perspective God was a Loving Parent who tenderly provided, cared for, and nurtured her own growth and that of all members of the human family.

Elizabeth wrote at a time when standard conventions did not yet exist for spelling, punctuation, and grammar. While the essence of Elizabeth's thoughts and sentence construction has been preserved in the selections quoted from her writings, some minor editorial changes have been made for comprehension by modern readers. In some instances outdated language has been replaced with current usage and omitted words have been added for clarity. Every effort has been made to preserve the integrity of the original text, including Elizabeth's choice of words, her peculiar phraseology, and the odd way she sometimes expressed her thoughts, even though these may not be in complete sentences.

Elizabeth habitually emphasized her written thoughts through the use of capitalization, underlining, or by the use of larger letters written more boldly. In the majority of such instances the use of italics in this text highlights the emphases made by Elizabeth in her own hand in the original. In some cases her capitalization has been retained.

Some names of places and individuals appear in several forms in the Seton documents. In this work, proper names of persons who lived in the United States have been anglicized but locations outside of America are in their original form, except for Livorno, Italy, which appears as "Leghorn" in this book. All biblical citations refer to post-Vatican II Catholic translations and numbering of the psalms.

God led Elizabeth Bayley Seton through the shipwreck of early blessings and a sea of sorrows on this earth to enjoy the bliss of eternity. Like Elizabeth, we are nourished by the Word of God and the Eucharist along our own pilgrimage to God and heaven. May Elizabeth be a model whose life inspires us in our own quest for holiness.

Saint Elizabeth Ann Seton, pray for us!

> Faith lifts the staggering soul on one side,
> Hope supports it on the other,
> Experience says it must be—
> And love says let it be.

ELIZABETH SETON TO JULIA SITGREAVES SCOTT
MARCH 26, 1810

DAY ONE

Sacred Scripture: "My Hidden Treasure"

FOCUS POINT

God continually reveals the gentle kindness and graciousness of divine love to the human family through sacred Scripture. Reading and prayerful reflection on the Word of God nourishes one's personal relationship with the Creator. Regular meditation on sacred Scripture sustained Elizabeth throughout her life.

If to now you have been so unhappy as to be like a highway in which the precious seed of the word of God is trampled under foot by those who pass along, or like stone amongst which it cannot take root because it finds no earth or moisture, or like thorns which grow up so abundantly that they choke its plants.... If till now you have heard the word of God with dissipation and without any recollection, with indifference and insensibility, with a mind employed about a thousand trifles and useless thoughts, acknowledge humbly your fault. Ask pardon from your God. Entreat his goodness most earnestly to stop your volatile mind, to mollify your heart so unfaithful to his grace, to disengage it from vain things which engage all your attention. In a word to make it like good soil which may preserve the good seed, foster it, and bring forth its fruits a hundred fold (Elizabeth Seton, Instruction on the Word of God, 17).

L ike the parable of the Sower, Jesus invites his listeners to attend to the many ways God speaks to members of the human family and invites them into discipleship (see Matthew 13:1–9). God chooses to reveal his loving care for creation in diverse ways, sometimes obvious and at other times, more subtle. The Holy Spirit may be present in the gentle summer breezes of youthful hearts or in the roaring winds of trials in maturity. Elizabeth's awareness of the active presence of God drew her into an ever deeper personal relationship with God.

Elizabeth invites us to be life-giving persons who, like "good soil," nurture the growth of God's word and are nourished by it. In living the Christian life in this way we become instruments of God who actualize the divine plan in our world. Elizabeth gives us an example of steadfast love in her roles as wife, mother, widow, and religious woman. Regardless of trials, she remains a woman of peace. Her watch of the heart and thirst for the Divine moved her to biblically inspired prayer. This lifelong practice permeated her being and all her actions.

THE LORD IS MY SHEPHERD

Among the earliest memories of Elizabeth's lonely childhood was one of being taught Psalm 23 by her stepmother. In her journal entitled "Dear Remembrances," Elizabeth wrote "'the Lord is my Shepherd, the Lord ruleth me'—and all through life it has been the favorite Psalm 'though I walk in the midst of the Shadow of

Death, I will fear no evil, for thou art with me'" (*SW*, 345; see also Ps 23:4).

Elizabeth learned from experiences in her childhood to trust God firmly. At that time she first knew the terror of uncertainty. At age twelve she spent a night "in the sweat of terror saying all the while OUR FATHER." Fear, insecurity, and anxiety about the future were not unknown to Elizabeth who was also protected from injury due to mob violence in lower Manhattan during the Doctors Riot of 1788 and the Highbinders Riot of Christmas Eve in 1806. Prayer was Elizabeth's source of strength and consolation during these trials. The same must be true for us today.

Looking beyond the pain of her immediate circumstance, Elizabeth viewed her reality in light of eternal life with her loving Creator. She is a model for us on our journey of faith. Her example invites us to be ever conscious of the unending care of Divine Providence. Elizabeth invites us to acknowledge our fears in the face of threatening situations and events. In all circumstances there is a mysterious potential of grace. As people of faith, we know that God is always with us.

Scarred by early maternal loss, Elizabeth valued meaningful and close relationships. Despite family conflicts, Elizabeth experienced God's unconditional and loving acceptance. Elizabeth placed her abiding trust in Divine Providence which to her was an expression of God's redeeming love and the graciousness of the Father of all. Elizabeth, with her heart oriented heavenward, lived her life conversant with the One she loved (see *EBS*, 464).

Elizabeth created sacred space in her day and prioritized her tasks so that reading the Bible became part of her daily routine. Fearless throughout life, Elizabeth treasured her Bible. Its consoling passages moved her to bare her soul to her Creator in all humility: "O my God! *Forgive* what I have been, *correct* what I am, and *direct* what I shall be. From break of day I seek thee, till the dead of night—All is solitary where thou are not, and where thou art is fullness of joy" (*SW*, 340).

AN UNFAILING COMFORT

As a busy wife and mother of young children, who were often sick, Elizabeth found time for spiritual reading which was a source of "continual enjoyment" for her, especially the "dear Scriptures" (CW, 250). It was her habitual practice to read the books of the Bible in rotation. In this way she familiarized herself with the key biblical figures and their stories, retelling them to all whom she instructed. When her husband was away on business travels, Elizabeth would take her bible and read until she fell asleep.

When she traveled to Italy with her ill husband, it was a blessing that Elizabeth had the presence of mind to pack her bible and scriptural commentaries in their baggage. During the Setons' futile journey to restore her husband's rapidly declining health, these texts provided great comfort to them. She kept her bible ever in view and turned to it for both inspiration and consolation. For Elizabeth, her "hidden treasure" was the Word of God (EBS, 244).

Through its powerful passages, she came to know her heavenly Father in new and surprising ways as God's plan for her unfolded through human events. During the dismal days of detention while the Setons were quarantined, reading the Bible became almost the only source of solace for Elizabeth and her husband. The uplifting message of the Word of God eased their spirits. "Indeed our reading is an unfailing comfort" (EBS, 271). Biblical passages lifted them into the sacred spheres of faith and hope.

For Elizabeth, this time was a crucible of purification for spiritual growth. For her husband, their ordeal provoked a personal conversion which prepared him to meet his Maker in peace.

Elizabeth found particular psalms especially meaningful in her mature years, particularly Psalms 42 and 84. These made her realize "how the saints died of love and joy" (ASJPH 12:44). She prayerfully pondered the psalms in the traditional fashion of meditative reading of the Bible, or *lectio divina*. Contemplative praying of the Word of God became a means for Elizabeth to deepen her relationship with God. As she considered the significance of particular passages, she must have often asked herself some of the following questions. "What is God saying to me?" "What am

I prompted to say to God?" "What difference can this biblical text make in my life?"

DIRECT WHAT I SHALL BE

In living her baptismal commitment Elizabeth radiated gospel values which she culled from reading her bible. For her it was a text of life and her travel guide for her pilgrimage on this earth. The Bible led Elizabeth to ponder God's call in her heart. Her familiarity with sacred Scripture prepared her for her life's mission. Through the pages of sacred Scripture Elizabeth met her God and came to know her deepest self, often discovering the shadow of her own human frailty. Seeking God and the kingdom of heaven were her priorities (see Matthew 6:31–33).

Among Elizabeth's daily prayers were the following: a prayer of repentance (Psalm 51), the great prayer of praise (*Te Deum*), and in her later years, the canticle of Mary (*Magnificat*). Elizabeth's poems, prayers, and books of meditations and instructions are steeped in sacred Scripture. Reading about the prophets and their expectation for Israel brought Elizabeth into communion with Mary the Mother of God whose "own piety and secret thoughts and prayers" had dwelt upon the very same passages (*SRP*, 103).

Journaling about religious experiences was a means of self-expression for Elizabeth. Sometimes she shared her religious reflections with kindred souls. In touch with the full spectrum of her human emotions and their rhythmic waves, both solitude and friendships were life-giving for Elizabeth. She was a person whose heart was easily moved to tears and who expressed her feelings freely—to God and those around her. She was moved when praying "our two divine Psalms 103 [Praise of Divine Goodness] and 104 [Praise of God the Creator]" and adds that her "tears [were] mixed on the Bible."

With her pen Elizabeth marked passages which impressed her as a way of highlighting special inspirations of the Spirit for later reflection and prayer, particularly in the Book of Isaiah and the Gospel of Luke. Such can be a useful practice for our own growth in praying with sacred Scripture. From her markings of passages dealing with eternity, peace, blessings, weeping, and silence one may gain some insight into Elizabeth's spiritual horizon and dominant themes which were important to her.

Elizabeth exhorted the members of her community "to read twenty-five verses of the New Testament on their knees" during a brief period of prayer before the noon meal. Have I found the practice of daily reading of sacred Scripture beneficial in my spiritual life?

REFLECTION QUESTIONS

How does reading the Sacred Scripture help me to grow spiritually? In the midst of my activities what helps me to create sacred space to prayerfully read and reflect on sacred Scripture? What biblical passages touch my heart most powerfully, drawing me into intimacy with God? How do I allow the Word of God to enlighten me? To what is God calling me at this time in my life? How am I responding to this invitation? What stepping stones of faith has God placed in the path of my life? In the spirit of Elizabeth, in what ways does the Good Shepherd provide for me?

DAY TWO

Divine Providence:
"Every Good Promise of God"

FOCUS POINT

Through the choices they make, members of the human family reflect the loving solicitude of Divine Providence in all their relations with one another. In choosing to live by gospel values one collaborates with the divine plan through prayer, suffering, and acts of charity. Elizabeth Seton chose to live her life for others through a preferential love for orphans, widows, and her neighbor in need (see Matthew 25:35–40).

You know the general principle—that God is everywhere—on the throne of his glory and among the blessed, but also throughout the whole Universe which he fills, governs, and preserves, ruling it by his wisdom and power. This we learn in our infancy. We learn it as an act of memory in childhood, yet in the practice of life, we live day by day as if we scarcely remembered that God

*sees us. God is so infinitely present to us that he is in every part of
our life and being—nothing can separate us from him. He is more
intimately present to us than we are to ourselves, and whatever
we do is done in him (Elizabeth Seton, On the Exercise of the
Presence of God (n.d.), 1).*

God encircled Elizabeth with divine love and provided for her
welfare with unending attentiveness. For her God was
ever-present. Elizabeth grew in the spiritual life through attentiveness to the presence of God within and around her. She believed that "we become enriched with the gifts of his grace which
will obtain us those of his glory, and after living in his presence
and love we will die thinking of him and loving him" (*EPG*, 13).

Elizabeth saw Christ in her neighbor. Her incarnational encounters with God led her into a communion of heart with the
Divine through service to the least of her brothers and sisters (see
Matthew 25:40). Elizabeth's belief in the promise and abiding
love of God was a source of consolation for herself and those
with whom she shared her religious ideals. She advised her youngest sister-in-law to make learning about God her chief study since
"it is the only knowledge which can fill the heart with a peace
and joy, which nothing can disturb" (*EBS*, 214).

NEITHER SLUMBERS NOR SLEEPS

Elizabeth relied confidently on Divine Providence. In her journal,
"Dear Remembrances," she recalled that from her youth she
viewed God as "Father" and placed herself at the mercy of God's
gracious care. When struggling with adolescence in the midst of
her father's marital problems in his second marriage, a miserable
Elizabeth became distraught emotionally by inner conflicts and
was sorely tempted to take an overdose of an opium-derivative
drug (laudanum).

She wrote with relief in "Dear Remembrances" of her horror

at her own distorted thinking about "every good promise of God," expressing her "praise and thanks of excessive joy not to have done the horrid deed." Filled with remorse, she writes of her "thousand promises of ETERNAL GRATITUDE" (SW, 346). Like Elizabeth, we are often tempted to abandon trust in God's loving Providence but do we pause to express our gratitude to God for the loving protection of Divine Providence?

A more mature Elizabeth some years later wrote her close friend Eliza Craig Sadler: "There is a Providence which neither slumbers nor sleeps" (EBS, 9). Elizabeth had grown in the realization that God would provide tenderly for her despite the tensions in her extended family which were swirling around her at that time. She remained serene "whatever might happen." The realization of God's eternal vigilance over creation which had dawned earlier gradually developed over time. This conviction deepened and remained a guiding light throughout the rest of Elizabeth's life.

As a wife concerned for her husband's welfare, especially when he was away on business trips, she wrote him that she "must trust [in] that Mercy which alone can preserve you from every danger" (EBS, 7). Elizabeth truly found God everywhere—in people, in events, and in circumstances: "Our good God has his times and moments for every thing" (November 20, 1814).

An attitude of gratitude characterized Elizabeth in all her relationships. Her friend Antonio Filicchi often spoke of "a most gracious Providence" that cared for the needs of the human family. With a deep sense of gratitude for God's benevolent care, Elizabeth exclaimed, "Oh, with what a thankful soul I shall adore that Providence" (EBS, 354).

TIDE OF PROVIDENCE

Early in her life Elizabeth realized how much she relied on God's promise and counted on the constancy of divine love amid variations in human feelings. The embrace of God was comforting, protecting, and tender for her. She experienced an inner divine consolation during the harsh weeks she was quarantined with her ill husband in the lazaretto: "My Father and my God—who by the consoling voice of his Word, builds up the Soul in hope, so as to free it (even for hours) of its encumbrances—confirming and strengthening it by the hourly experience of his indulgent goodness" (*EBS*, 267).

Even in the midst of her struggles to establish the Sisters of Charity, Elizabeth gave thanks for her blessings. At that time she wrote George Weis, a friend, that her "mouth waters" at the thought of God's favors "but let all be in the order of His Providence neither asking nor refusing" (August 9, 1810). From the Source of Mercy flowed sustaining grace which gave Elizabeth "new life in Him even while in the midst of sorrows and care—sustaining, directing, consoling" (*EBS*, 267). Elizabeth reminds us that we are the face, hands, and touch of God for others. In what ways do we convey the love, compassion, and hospitality of God to those around us?

Elizabeth advised her son William in an undated letter early in 1817 that the limited provision men and women make for the future may be altered in a flash "since the Providence of God turns out so often quite different from our calculations." She had learned that when one door closes, God opens another. It was while traveling to Italy with her husband for his health that Elizabeth met the Filicchi family in Leghorn and was introduced to Roman Catholicism. The events, circumstances, and timing of our lives, like Elizabeth's, emanate from the same Source of providential care.

Elizabeth became increasingly attentive to the many epiphanies of God around her. Her encounters with Providence sensitized her to the active evolution of God's plan in her life. The moments of grace which touched the heart of Elizabeth added to the wellspring of faith and courage in her soul. Elizabeth's vision focused on another horizon—her future of eternal life. Chiding her eldest son, she wrote, "You say *tide of fate*…but I say *tide of providence* which [is] as infinite goodness" (March 1818). With an eye toward eternity Elizabeth gave thanks for God's active goodness in her life.

IMPULSE OF GRACE

Elizabeth praised God as the "merciful giver" of "unspeakable blessings" and for the "blessed impulse of Grace" which she wished for those she loved most (*EBS*, 180). She saw her relationship with God as "the means of Grace and comfort" on earth and as a prelude to "pleasure and joy thro' Eternity" (*EBS*, 180). Living her baptismal commitment deeply, Elizabeth shared her spiritual fervor with others.

Before departing for Italy, Elizabeth penned farewell sentiments to her beloved sister-in-law Rebecca Seton, whom she called her "soul sister." "May the Divine Spirit strengthen your *soul* in His service and make your way plain before you. Whatever are the changes in this our mortal life, may we find our rest in that Blessed Fold where dear friends will no more be separated" (*EBS*, 224). Tuberculosis took Rebecca, 23, to her eternal life within weeks of Elizabeth's return to New York.

Later in Maryland, as she pondered the prospect of forming a community committed to charitable service and the education of young women in the faith, Elizabeth formed a vision of mission rather than a business plan. The details of her future were uncertain, but her conviction about it was firm. She shared her thoughts with Antonio Filicchi: "There is every hope that it [her school in Baltimore] will gradually succeed, as it is committed solely to [the] providence of Almighty God.... I must trust all to Divine Providence" (July 8, 1808).

The Sisters of Charity, her spiritual daughters, were impelled by the love of Christ to carry out their mission of charity (see 1 John 4:21; 2 Cor 5:14.) Elizabeth's Episcopalian roots had nourished her heart with a familiarity for the richness of biblical passages. Elizabeth advised Cecilia O'Conway, the first Sister of Charity, to be careful to meet her grace in opportunities which came her way. Elizabeth believed that providential circumstances contained a treasury of grace awaiting one's acceptance (see *SW*, 303).

Firmly trusting God's promise despite distressing circumstances, Elizabeth believed in God's eternal love for all of creation and wrote to her lifelong friend, Julianna Sitgreaves Scott, whom she affectionately simply called "Julia": "God will provide, that is all my comfort never did that Providence fail me" (December 15, 1813). As a poverty-stricken widow, unemployed and homeless, Elizabeth experienced the benevolence of charitable persons who responded with compassion to her impoverished situation.

REFLECTION QUESTIONS

Do I believe in Divine Providence? What pivotal event(s) or moment(s) of grace most clearly reveal the working of Divine Providence in my journey of faith? How has God used me as an instrument of Divine Providence to bring hope, compassion, and care to people in need? What helps me to discover the store of grace awaiting me in the midst of unexpected changes in my life? In the spirit of Elizabeth, what must I do to meet my grace?

DAY THREE

Family Bonds: "My Turn at Dancing"

FOCUS POINT

Jesus gave his disciples a framework for making choices and building strong family bonds (see Matthew 5: 31–32). These teachings invite men and women to live by gospel values as family members, parishioners, and citizens in society. Elizabeth Seton was a living reflection of the compassionate face of Christ to persons in need. She believed in God's promises. Her life gave witness to those around her of the One who is the Eternal Promise.

You said a word to me about dancing—I don't know much of the style of the present day, but when I was young I never found any effect from it but the most innocent cheerfulness both in public and private. I remember remorse of conscience about so much time lost in it, and my trouble at being so unable to say my prayers seeing always my partners instead of my God...also my vexation at the time it took to prepare dresses for balls, but cannot remember the least indecency or pride in dress, or the smallest familiarity or impropriety in dancing which, in truth, if you will consider it as a good exercise and if you must be in company, preferable to private chitchat (Mother's Advices to Her Daughter, Catherine Josephine Seton (n.d.), 19).

E lizabeth knew the sadness of early parental loss. Not yet three years of age when her mother died, Elizabeth's father was a better physician than parent. She knew years of loneliness as a result of her his second marriage. Her stepmother preferred her own seven children. The shadow of these experiences framed Elizabeth's adolescent dreams for a brighter future. God alone became her consolation.

Delighted to be courted by the popular William Magee Seton, Elizabeth was "perfectly happy" when she could "enjoy the Society of her Friend" (*EBS*, 2). She was a belle of the balls of New York and light on her feet in monogrammed satin dancing slippers with sharply pointed toes. Her vibrancy reveals itself in her letters, in which Elizabeth makes recurring references to dancing, such as taking her "turn at dancing," and "the very thought [of a close relationship with God] sets the very soul dancing" (To Julia Scott, December 2, 1811; December 15, 1813). The dance of Elizabeth's life focused on her divine Partner.

DREAMS OF PLEASURE

Elizabeth's years growing up were permeated with youthful longings and wistful dreams of future pleasure. Elizabeth spent almost half of her young life away from her father's home living with relatives. At times she felt disconnected and rejected. These feelings fed into her adolescent conflicts growing up. In "Mother's Advices," a journal written for Catherine (Kitty) Seton, Elizabeth poignantly reminded her second daughter that she herself, "poor,

poor Betsy Bayley had no Mother, nor even principles to keep her from folly" (*MA*, 17).

Her earliest memories were sad ones. She longed for both acceptance and harmony within the Bayley household where the two sets of Bayley offspring never blended well as a family. Elizabeth spent long periods of time in her girlhood living by the Long Island Sound where she enjoyed the solitude of beach combing and exploring nature along the sand dunes. When Elizabeth was sixteen, she became acutely aware of her father's marital problems with her stepmother. She could not understand "why when I spoke kindly to relations, they did not speak to me; and could not even guess how any one could be an enemy to another" (*SW*, 346).

During adolescence Elizabeth had an innate bent toward introspection. She described herself as follows: "There is a certain temper I am sometimes subject to—it is not sullenness or absolute discontent, 'tis a kind of melancholy; still I like it better than those effusions of cheerfulness, that hilarity of spirits, which a good night's rest and a fine morning often inspire. I prefer the sadness, because I know it may be removed; it may change to cheerfulness. The gaiety, I am sure, will change to sadness before the day ends. And perhaps to sorrow; 'tis not the natural temper, but the influence of situation. I trust the day may come when I shall show a more regular and Christian disposition. Perhaps it may; it may not. Those passions must be governed" *(MS, 5)*.

Such insights enabled Elizabeth in later years to comfort pupils who were struggling with emotions arising from painful situations in their families of origin. What have been the patterns of my life and how have these influenced me?

Although at eighteen she dreamed of "fine plans of a little country home, to gather all the little children round and teach them their prayers, and keep them clean and teach them to be good," that didn't happen according to her fantasy (*SW*, 346). Instead Elizabeth became the wife of the prominent William Magee Seton. Within eight years of her marriage Elizabeth gave birth to three daughters and two sons.

INDESCRIBABLE SATISFACTION

Elizabeth knew both rejection and reconciliation. The emotional distance surrounding the relationship with her stepmother seems to have been a recurring theme for Elizabeth. No facts are known about the conflict between Dr. Bayley and his second wife. Eventually the Bayleys separated after twenty-one years of marriage. From her own experience Elizabeth knew the complications of blended families, remorse, and the price of unconditional love. She also learned that one must wait for the tides of time and grace to heal wounds and mend relationships according to God's terms.

Elizabeth waited. She learned that God's love touches hearts at different times and in various ways. After she returned from Italy, Mrs. Bayley, also a widow by this time, reached out to the widowed Elizabeth. Her gesture touched Elizabeth deeply. Writing to her lifelong friend Julia Sitgreaves Scott, Elizabeth shared her sentiments on the improvement in their relationship. "I believe I have expressed to you my pleasure in receiving from her since my return home every mark of peace and reconciliation, which also gives me the double enjoyment of the confidence and affection" of her youngest half-sisters, Helen [15] and Mary [14] (EBS, 384).

The reconciliation must have been permeated with the grace of forgiveness and some insight into the causes of their fractured family bonds. Providentially, at the height of the storm surrounding her conversion to Roman Catholicism, Elizabeth was summoned to attend the last hours of her stepmother. This required her to spend many days at Charlotte Bayley's bedside, providing time for healing old wounds. That experience was one of "indescribable satisfaction" (EBS, 384).

Elizabeth realized that she was the one God used to bring consolation to her stepmother. In the mysterious ways of God, the dying woman had shaped Elizabeth's personality and spirituality. She had taught Elizabeth her first prayers and played a significant role in Elizabeth becoming who she was as an adult and as a future saint.

Elizabeth expressed her heartfelt gratitude for the many ways the Catholic Church ministers to persons who are dying. She wrote

Antonio Filicchi about her distress that "these poor souls die without Sacraments, without prayers, and left in their last moments to the conflicts of parting nature" (*EBS*, 385). She was so grateful for "the divine consolations which our Almighty God has so mercifully provided" for Catholics and filled with hope "for the different prospect" she anticipated for herself "in that hour through the divine goodness and mercy" (*EBS*, 385).

THE VERY SOUL DANCING

Elizabeth grew spiritually as a loving wife; she and William Magee shared happiness despite illness, death, business reversals, and ultimately bankruptcy. Yet, through it all, Elizabeth, the ever loving wife and devoted mother, managed to retain her equilibrium and courageously supported her husband in his desperate fight to regain his health and salvage the family mercantile firm.

When he was away on business, Elizabeth felt his absence keenly and wrote him about her concerns which included "the idea of the inconveniences you may be suffering, while these arms, *heart,* and bed are all forlorn without you" (*EBS*, 6). Just after his departure on another trip, she hastily sent him these poignant lines. "Your Darlings have enjoyed this cool day and are merry as birds. They cannot understand that Papa is not to come [neither today] nor tomorrow, nor the next day, nor the day after—that is for their Mother to feel" (*EBS*, 231).

The Setons' charmed life of prosperity soon encountered reversals. Elizabeth spent herself tirelessly supporting her husband but William Magee shared little about himself with her and soon became despondent. His health grew increasingly precarious. The public embarrassment of pending financial ruin was humiliating and the uncertainty became a source of anxiety for the family. The family business failed as a result of war abroad and piracy on the high seas. The firm went bankrupt. The Setons lost their home and possessions at the same time that tuberculosis eroded William Magee's health. Elizabeth referred to this period as their "worldly shipwreck" (*EBS*, 418).

Fearing that her husband might be imprisoned for his debts, Elizabeth recoiled. "That is a nerve that shrinks from the touch." For her, "Faith and Hope" became her "only refuge" in the midst of the year-long storm of anxious anticipation of a solution (*EBS*, 140). Yet, with her beliefs in the blessings of a God who sustains all, Elizabeth gave thanks that her children remained in good health while her "own strength of mind" increased "with the storm" (*EBS*, 140).

Elizabeth's God-centered vision colored her views of the trials of life. Over time the divine Lover had the last dance with Elizabeth. In later years she described an inner experience with her eucharistic Lord: "All the excesses of my heart found their play and it danced with more fervor" after receiving holy Communion (*EBS*, 377). The Eucharist nourished Elizabeth on her earthly pilgrimage. Her faith enabled her to dance to the inner rhythm of divine love, anticipating the Eternal Dance in union with the Trinity. As Elizabeth later explained to Julia Sitgreaves Scott, "the very thought sets the very Soul dancing" and "every thing else is like the flying clouds" enabling her to "jump over all the troubles of this life with more gaiety and real lightness of heart than" could be imagined without believing in the God of Promise (December 15, 1813).

REFLECTION QUESTIONS

Are family bonds and relationships important to me? Why? What are some of the recurring themes in my life? How does the God of Promise bring healing to my personal scars? How does prayer enable me to focus my energies on the things that really matter? What makes me feel like dancing to the inner rhythm of divine love? How are the whisperings of the Spirit calling me to live gospel values in my daily life? To be a person of mercy, charity, and justice? In the spirit of Elizabeth, how am I facing the future which may bring adversity or prosperity?

DAY FOUR

Parenthood: "A Mother's Heart"

FOCUS POINT

Parents who provide religious education for their children make it possible for their faith to develop so that they become responsible adults whose lives of Christlike virtue may radiate gospel values. Elizabeth Seton was first and foremost a mother who formed her children in the ways of God. When considering the establishment of the Sisters of Charity, Elizabeth declared that she would "gladly make every sacrifice…consistent with my first and inseparable obligations as a Mother" (*SW*, 274).

I will tell you in what I know American parents to be most difficult—in hearing the faults of their children. In twenty instances where you see the faults, they are not to be immediately corrected by the parents, but rather by good advices and education. It is best not to speak of them to Papa and Mamma, who feel as if you reflected on their very selves. While to you [teachers and caretakers] the parents will say, "Yes, Sir, I know, I perceive," in the heart they think it is not so much; and they will soften and excuse to the child, what they condemn to us. Our efforts afterwards avail very little—so that is a big point (Elizabeth Seton to Simon Gabriel Bruté, January 1816).

Elizabeth's life was about nurturing the human and spiritual development of others. Elizabeth understood the biblical admonition to transmit family values: "Take care and be earnestly on your guard not to forget the things which your own eyes have seen…but teach them to your children and to your children's children" (Deuteronomy 4:9). Yet, in so doing she was realistic in assessing the temperaments and personal limitations of her own children.

In dealing with the parents of her pupils, Elizabeth admitted that "a Mother sees through a veil which renders the object as she wishes it" (*EBS*, 16). As an educator, Elizabeth approached her students and their families with a mother's heart. She was open to their unique personalities, accepted differences, and affirmed their least efforts. This attitude permeated all her relationships. Her goal was to prepare them for the world in which they were destined to live. Her experiences as a mother, widow, and sole parent equipped her to understand the challenges of parenthood and the need for sensitivity to each person.

MY DARLINGS

In her reminiscences Elizabeth fondly recalled her happy years as a wife and mother. Born to nurture others, Elizabeth, who herself had been deprived of familial closeness growing up, created a home built on love and mutual affection. She loved babies and enjoyed being a mother, although she almost died in giving birth to her third child.

At a time when she had only three preschoolers, Elizabeth wrote her close friend Eliza Craig Sadler that "the Darlings are too precious, too lovely, and their mother too happy" (*EBS*, 81). Openly affectionate, in letters to her many friends, Elizabeth often sent them "a thousand kisses from the Darlings" (*EBS*, 93).

Yet, like so many other parents, the Setons had their fair share of parental dilemmas over child rearing practices. They were also well acquainted with toddlers' tantrums. When Anna Maria was just two years old, her honest mother confessed that her oldest "does not possess those gentle expressions of sensibility.... I only have the least influence with her, because her disposition is exactly my own," referring to the fiery temperament characteristic of the Bayleys (*EBS*, 16).

In her frustration about managing Anna Maria, Elizabeth consulted a family friend about childhood discipline. Elizabeth explained that her daughter "possesses from her Mother a most ungovernable temper and with all my endeavors is past all management. My William leaves her to me, My Father tells me, conquer her by gentleness. Wright Post and my sister recommend *Whipping*, which is to me an unnatural resource, and the last I shall have recourse to" (*CW*, 1:17). She concluded her letter by adding the following urgent request. "Send me a word of advice on this subject, or rather make haste to set me right, and assist me in a case which demands more resolution than any situation I have hitherto experienced" (*CW*, 1:17).

Elizabeth soon developed her own style of parenting which included brief but tender notes for her children when she was away from them. In one written as she embarked for Italy, Elizabeth reassured her five-year-old son Richard that "Mamma longs to kiss you and hold you in her arms." The knowing mother also exhorted the boy to be helpful toward his younger sister. "Take care of Kitty and do not do any thing to vex her, if you love me" (*EBS*, 241).

Being a mother always requires self-sacrifice, patience, and respect for each child. Elizabeth had ample opportunity to practice these virtues as she listened to each one's prattle: "My companions talk so fast they confuse my brain" (*EBS*, 93). Yet, Elizabeth, like Jesus, welcomed their playful surprises because "the kingdom of heaven belongs to such as these" (Matthew 19:14).

WHOLLY DEPENDENT

The recent widow visited her husband's grave and "wept plentifully over it with unrestrained affection," recalling the pain and paradox of the "last sufferings of his life added to remembrance of former *years*" which made his memory "more than precious" (*EBS*, 294). In her grief, Elizabeth records her pain in a journal for her sister-in-law. "When you read my daily memorandums since I left home you will feel what my love has been, and acknowledge that God alone could support my soul thro' such proofs as has been required of it" (*EBS*, 294).

After Elizabeth's return to New York it was humiliating for her to rely on the charity of others during the first year of her widowhood. "My Seton has left his five darlings and myself wholly dependent" and if the kindness of some relatives who respected him "did not continue to be faithful friends to us, I should see my dear ones in a state of absolute poverty" (*EBS*, 313). She explored various alternatives for employment but none seemed feasible: "Some proposals have been made me of keeping a tea store, or China Shop, or *small* school for little children (too young I suppose to be taught the 'Hail Mary'). In short…they do not know what to do with me, but God does and when His blessed time comes we shall know" (*EBS*, 394).

Despite her impoverishment, the sole parent of five young children, all under eight years of age, Elizabeth rejoiced in being able to have a roof over their heads. Her desire to start a school was blocked by religious bigotry. Her employment as a teacher ended abruptly when her employer's school failed financially. Next she cared for boys attending a nearby boarding school until some of the parents became dissatisfied and withdrew their sons from her care. That diminished the Setons' income and required them to move to lower income housing.

Elizabeth neither begrudged nor resented her new station in life, but accepted it with composure and fortitude. Hiring others for washing and mending had been her former practice but in her widowhood Elizabeth found that such mundane domestic tasks affirmed her sense of self-worth in "the pleasure of doing something for my Darlings [which] makes every labor easy" (*EBS*, 397). In a letter to a close friend, Elizabeth summed up her situation with faith-filled hope. "I have been constantly busy with my Darlings mending, hemming, and turning winter clothes. They have in turn all been sick from the change of weather, added to their whooping cough...in short, dear, I have been one of Job's sisters, and from all appearances must long look to his example. Well, I am satisfied—to sow in tears if I may reap in joy. When all the wintry storms of time are past, we shall enjoy the delights of an Eternal Spring" (*EBS*, 335).

I AM A MOTHER

Valiantly parenting alone, Elizabeth's maternal pride in the accomplishments of her children was justified. "Kit [5] is the gayest little being you can imagine with a very quick capacity—Rebecca [3] is doted on by us all.... Anna [10] will attend an excellent dancing Master...not for the steps, but to obtain a little polish" (*EBS*, 397). While William [8] and Richard [6] were living with their mother among the boarders under her charge, everyone found the situation difficult, including Elizabeth who expressed her exasperation in a letter to Julia Sitgreaves Scott: "My saucy Boys almost master me" (*EBS*, 361).

Elizabeth, who understood the challenges of parenting, was strengthened in her resolve about the sacredness of her maternal obligations as the sole parent. In all things, Elizabeth looked to the heavens appealing to Divine Providence. In every situation and in all the choices Elizabeth made, her priority was always, first and foremost, her children and their best interests. Her motherly concerns ranged from secular to spiritual, temporal to eternal, and related primarily to issues of education and salvation.

As her sons matured and left Saint Joseph's Valley for apprenticeships and life experience, she continued her maternal vigilance for their welfare. When William was studying commerce with the Filicchis in Italy, she wrote him: "My own son, be blessed with the full blessing of a Mother's heart, think how it dotes on you and how I have held you in it all these heavenly feasts" (June 10, 1816).

At the time of her conversion, she offered this explanation to Amabilia Baragazzi Filicchi: "Now they tell me to take care because *I am a Mother*. I must answer for my children in Judgment, whatever Faith I lead them to" (*EBS*, 374). In her search for the true faith, Elizabeth initially was unconscious about how her choice of religion would be so consequential for both herself and her children. Later as a Catholic in Maryland, she reiterated her commitment to her obligations of motherhood but remained open to accept and say "Amen" to the unfolding of God's plan through Divine Providence.

After burying Anna Maria, her oldest, at sixteen, Elizabeth referred to herself as "a hard hearted Mother" in a letter to her lifelong friend Julia Sitgreaves Scott (August 11, 1813). By this time Elizabeth was well seasoned with sorrows. She confided her sober thoughts to Julia about the long-term best interests of the remaining Seton children. May they "fight it [life] out as their Mother did before them, looking to Providence and beyond the grave.... Well I hope they will be punished by disappointments and adversity till they do" (11 August 1813). She was preoccupied with the spiritual welfare of her children as she also enabled others to grow in relationship with God.

REFLECTION QUESTIONS

Do I convey the tenderness of God's parental love to others? How am I called to support others in their need? What challenges do widows, widowers, and sole parents face in fulfilling their parental obligations alone? What are some supports which nourish one's inner resources in fulfilling this difficult role? What qualities of a loving parent's heart does God invite me to deepen and express more freely? What is God inviting me to nurture in my own life? In the spirit of Elizabeth, in what ways is God urging me to grow spiritually and help others live by gospel values?

DAY FIVE

The Will of God: "Hope Always Awake"

FOCUS POINT

Like Christ, believers are called to do the will of God (see Matthew 26:42). The Holy Spirit leads the people of God to deepen their understanding of faith as a framework for all their actions. This lifelong process involves listening to the Spirit within and around us. Elizabeth Seton took her call to discipleship seriously seeking to do God's will. She had an abiding awareness of God's presence and action in her life and allowed the Spirit to transform her in prayer.

I hope you continue to be good after all your fiery trials. Three times a week I beg for you with my whole Soul in the hour of favor when nothing is denied to Faith. Imagine your poor little wandering erring Sister standing on the Rock, and admitted so often to the spring of Eternal Life—the healing balm of every wound. Indeed if I wore a galling chain and lived on bread and water, I ought to feel the transport of grace, but Peace of Mind and a sufficient share of exterior comfort with the inexhaustible Treasure keeps My Soul in a state of constant comparison between the Giver and receiver, the former days and the present. Hope always awake whispers Mercy for the future, as sure as in the past (Elizabeth Seton to Antonio Filicchi, June 22, 1807).

In her following of Christ, God's will was Elizabeth's compass. Her conscientious focus on knowing and fulfilling God's plan led her to listen to God's Word and respond. She cooperated with grace and was transformed. She discerned what was good and pleasing and perfect to God by maintaining a stance of listening to both the Spirit and others (see Romans 12:2). When she made new commitments, she trusted in the God who had led her to that moment. "If it succeeds I bless God, if [it] does not succeed...I bless God, because then it will be right that it should not succeed" (*SW*, 180).

Elizabeth's way of discipleship was one of total submission to the divine will in steadfast love and devoted service to the needs of others (see 1 Corinthians 15:58). Graces and insights derived from prayer brought Elizabeth to a deeper realization of what it means to be a Christian. She was riveted on the truth of God's Word and the deposit of faith found in Roman Catholicism. Elizabeth attained closeness with her Creator through attentiveness to the Spirit in her life. She strived to be in tune with the presence of God around her. For Elizabeth, God was always present.

MERCY FOR THE FUTURE

Elizabeth's life revolved around the touchstone of her spirituality, discerning and doing the will of God. Elizabeth's mind-set focused early on choosing to conform to God's plan for her. "God has given me a great deal to do, and I have always, and hope always, to prefer his Will to every wish of my own" *(EBS, 313)*.

When instructing others, Elizabeth used the familiar style with which she was most comfortable and posed this timeless question to her listeners: "What was the first rule of our dear Savior's life?" (*MS*, 222). Elizabeth responded to their answers by elaborating on the sentiments Jesus expressed in his Bread of Life discourse. "I came down from heaven not to do my own will but the will of the one who sent me" (John 6:38). Elizabeth sought to imitate Jesus in doing God's will.

Elizabeth proposed simply that the first goal of one's daily work was simply to seek and do God's will in all matters whether they be ordinary or extraordinary. Elizabeth was guided by several key principles in her quest for union with God. "The first end I propose in our daily work is to do the will of God; secondly, to do it in the manner He wills; and thirdly, to do it because it is His will" (*MS*, 222).

Elizabeth found God day by day in the monotony of her routine duties as well as in unforeseen circumstances. She found God in the schoolroom and the kitchen, as well as in their humble chapel and on the verdant heights of the Catoctin spur of the Blue Ridge Mountains near Emmitsburg. Elizabeth saw the face of Christ equally in the poor beggar, the rebellious pupil, and the fervent novice.

Like Elijah, Elizabeth waited on her own Horeb (Mount Sinai) for the Lord to pass by the mountain, but she met God neither in an earthquake nor in a fire but in a "tiny whispering sound" deep within her being (see 1 Kings 19:11–12). Centered in the stillness of prayer Elizabeth heard the gentle murmurs of her Beloved deep within her heart. Like Elizabeth, the Spirit of God whispers to us in the most unexpected times and places but are we attentive? Are we able to truly listen to God's message?

Elizabeth was a woman of integrity who lived what she preached to others. At the brink of her decisive move to Emmitsburg, Maryland, she wrote to her devoted friend, Filippo Filicchi. "God's blessed, blessed will be done…all is in God's hands. If I had a choice and my own will should decide in a moment, I would remain silent in God's hands. Oh, how sweet it is there to rest in perfect confidence" (February 8, 1809). How comfortable am I with living life on God's terms?

GIVER AND RECEIVER

Conversing with God in prayer enabled Elizabeth to be attentive to the mysterious and often surprising ways the Spirit worked in her life. Elizabeth sought to imitate the docile cooperation with God's plan of salvation (see Philippians 2:8). In her instructions she explained that the great object of all God's mysteries was to share divine life with humankind (see MS, 222). For Elizabeth the interior life meant the continuation of Christ the Redeemer's life in her soul.

In prayer Elizabeth developed a grace-filled relationship with God. She was open and responsive to God's action in her life. One could say that Elizabeth maintained a ready stance of availability toward the One she loved. When situations were particularly trying and hard to accept by human standards, her characteristic response was the following: "but my God knows best" (EBS, 148). This she firmly believed with all her heart.

Belief in her God sufficed for Elizabeth to surrender to God's loving plan regardless of what it cost her. Grace gifted her with a marvelous pliability in the ways of the Spirit. Her conversation with God dealt with her emotions, needs, conflicts, joys, and sorrows. Her prayer life, rooted in Scripture, expressed itself in liturgical celebrations, personal spiritual reading, journaling, poetry, and contemplative solitude. Her chapel was simple. At times her best meeting place with God was a green cathedral in the woods of Saint Joseph's Valley or nearby Saint Mary's Mountain.

A prayer of Pope Pius VII became a favorite during her last years on earth. "May the most just, the most high and the most amiable will of God be in all things fulfilled, praised, and exalted above all forever" (MS, 287). When she repeated these words on her deathbed, they were no longer merely a familiar formula but truly were the hallmark of herself as a disciple of Jesus Christ. Learning how to make the Sign of the Cross also opened up a world of new meaning for Elizabeth as did discovering the rich religious and artistic heritage of Italy.

The beauty of Florentine art overwhelmed her. She was struck by a large painting of another grieving mother, Miriam of Nazareth, whose son had just been crucified. Elizabeth found herself mesmerized by the sorrowful mother receiving her son's corpse. The impressions of this powerful experience imbedded themselves into Elizabeth's memory: "How hard it was to leave that picture. How often even in the few hours interval since I have seen it, I shut my eyes and recall it in imagination" (*EBS*, 287). What questions do I hear the Spirit whispering at the core of my being about my relationship with God?

PEACE OF MIND

Elizabeth's drive to do the will of God was rooted in her tremendous awareness of God's presence in her life. Her guiding principle was that "God is everywhere" and that we should "remember that *God sees us*" (*EPG*, 1). For Elizabeth, the Compassionate One was in every part of human life to such a degree that nothing could separate her from her beloved. She taught that God is closer to us than we are to ourselves.

In her prayerful pondering of God's goodness Elizabeth made connections between the parables of Jesus and the appeals of the Old Testament. For example, echoing the plea made to Jesus by the blind beggar who said, "Lord, please let me see" (Luke 18:41), Elizabeth encouraged her listeners to use the psalms to reflect on God's presence. For example, the Psalmist asks whether one can hide or escape from the Spirit of God (Psalm 139:7).

The needs of the human family are ever present before the Creator whose attentiveness never falters. The very visibility of created beings allows unending access to God's eternal love and merciful compassion for all persons. Through meditation one's relationship with God develops and intensifies bearing the fruit of inner peace. Elizabeth turned her loving attention to God in contemplative prayer.

God's tender love encircled Elizabeth. "As birds in changing their places find the air wherever they fly, and fish who live in the water are surrounded by their element wherever they swim, so wherever we go we must find God everywhere" (*EPG*, 1). The astounding receptivity to God's grace in her soul resulted from Elizabeth's sense of communion with God in her life. Surrounded by divine love, Elizabeth believed that God was "more within us than we are in ourselves."

Her lifelong certitude in God's providential care prompted Elizabeth to highlight this aspect of her relationship with God. She also taught others about it in an instruction from "On the Exercise of the Presence of God." In it she spoke of her penchant for entrusting her whole self and her budding mission of charity to "God [who] in his continual presence with us is our Father" (*EPG*, 1).

For Elizabeth, God was a "Father infinitely more tender than any earthly Father can be, a Father rich in mercies, ever ready to forget our faults when we detest them, and to be present at all our wants…he fills us with his mercies which are new every morning, he covers us with his wings, carries us on his shoulders, and cherishes us as a mother nurses the child of her bosom. Our names, says the prophet [Isaiah] are written in his hand and the hairs of our head he has even numbered" (*EPG*, 2; see also Isaiah 44:5). How attentive am I to the many ways the loving mercy of God is present in my life?

REFLECTION QUESTIONS

Is God's will the compass of my spiritual life? What helps me to know and do God's will in my life? What steps do I take to discern God's will before making important choices and decisions? How helpful do I find spiritual direction for my spiritual growth? What name do I call God in prayer? What helps me to recognize God's presence in my life? Do I listen to God in prayer? In Scripture? In the Eucharist? In the Church? In the spirit of Elizabeth, how am I responding as a person of faith to humble and honest discipleship?

DAY SIX

The Eucharist: "Real Presence"

FOCUS POINT

The Eucharist is "the source and summit of the Christian life" (*LG*, 11). Believers are invited to be persons of integrity who promote harmony on earth in a spirit of peace and justice as Elizabeth did. She was a woman sustained by the Real Presence of Jesus in the Blessed Sacrament and her reception of Jesus Christ in holy Communion. Her example calls us to heed the invitation of Jesus: "Do this in memory of me" (Luke 22:19).

How happy is that moment O divine JESUS! How pure is that Light! How ineffable is that Communion of your Blessings! (…) Ah! if one were faithful, if one never departed from You, if one knew how to preserve the Grace received, how happy would one be! Yet this is but a drop of the infinite Ocean of Blessings which You are one day to Communicate to men and women…. O! Soul of my Soul, what is my Soul and what Good can it have without possessing You? Life of my Life! What is my life when I do not live in You? Is it possible that my Heart is capable of possessing You? Of enjoying You all alone? (...) Can a creature be so elevated to repose in You, and after that depart from You? Lord, I do not know what I ought to say to You, but hear the Voice of my Love, and of my Misery. Live always in me, and let me live perpetually in You, and for You, as I live only by You (Elizabeth Ann Seton to Cecilia Seton, July 8, 1807).

A s a devout Episcopalian, Elizabeth was fed by her frequent reception of holy Communion which she believed was the symbolic presence of Christ in the bread and wine. In Italy she marveled that Catholics who "love God and live good, regular lives can go [to Communion] (tho' many do not do it) yet they can go, *every day*" (*EBS*, 297). As Elizabeth journeyed through life, like the disciples on the road to Emmaus, the longer she walked in the company of Jesus, the more she came to know him in the breaking of the bread (see Luke 24:30).

As a Roman Catholic, the Eucharist drew Elizabeth into "Divine Communion which neither absence nor Death (except the eternal) can destroy, the bond of Faith and Charity uniting All" (*EBS*, 470). Elizabeth was awestruck by the Real Presence of Jesus Christ in the Eucharist. She believed in his promise that those who eat and drink share divine life now and in eternity (see John 6:53–54). She marveled at the "wonders" of a single reception of holy Communion, and found herself perpetually full of longing expressed in her "abundance of good thoughts and desires." She questioned her preparedness: "Is indeed my soul ready? (...) Is my welcome ready?" (*CPR*, 44).

OCEAN OF BLESSINGS

Feeding on the Bread of Life provided Elizabeth spiritual nourishment for her journey of faith. "This Heavenly Bread of Angels removes my pains, my cares—warms, cheers, soothes, contents, and renews my whole being" (*EBS*, 478). The reception of her beloved redeemer filled Elizabeth with undying gratitude.

Elizabeth never forgot her first Communion. She had counted the hours expectantly with "the watch of the heart panting for the Supreme happiness it had so long desired—the Secret, the Mystery of Benediction—heavenly delight, bliss—inconceivable to angels" (*SW*, 350). Words were inadequate to express her desire but "faith burning" kept her alert "watching for morning dawn through broken slumbers" until at last she "saw the first rays of the sun on the cross of Saint Peter's steeple burnished so bright it seemed *that morning*." On that day of days her feet seemed not to touch the ground "every step of the two miles" (*SW*, 350) she walked to church.

Returning home to her five darlings with the "Treasure" of her soul, Elizabeth planted her usual kiss on her children, thrilled to be "bringing such a Master" to their "little dwelling" (*SW*, 350). In the Eucharist Elizabeth discovered God's pathway of salvation for her. The moment of encounter was one of exquisite happiness which she could not describe in mere words. Her exclamation, "How pure is that Light!" somewhat conveys the ecstasy of her soul (*EBS*, 448).

Elizabeth longed to be filled with the precious graces of the Eucharist which enabled her to become more and more the person the Lord wished her to be. She rejoiced with the gift of the Eucharist, calling it "but a drop of the infinite Ocean of Blessings" which God communicates to believers (*EBS*, 448). She expressed how she offered herself to God the Father through Jesus Christ and her union with him in the "Holy Spirit who is the Mutual Love of Both" (*EBS*, 448).

REAL PRESENCE

Elizabeth toured various historical and religious sites in Italy with the Filicchi family. She was overcome with the concept of the Real Presence when she visited the Shrine of Our Lady of Grace in the monastery of Montenero. During the sacred liturgy at that monastery shrine, Elizabeth experienced a defining moment in her spiritual journey.

Elizabeth recounted how she had blushed deeply at its powerful impact on her. "There this poor young Englishman at the very moment the priest was doing the most sacred action they [Roman Catholics] call the elevation...just at that moment this wild young man said loudly in my ear, 'This is what they call their *Real Presence*'" (*EBS*, 291). Elizabeth was shocked by the brazen boldness and disrespect of this individual, since she believed respect was due everyone in the matter of religion (see *EBS*, 290). Elizabeth held in high regard the dogmas and pious practices of others.

The incident touched Elizabeth to the core of her being, prompting an unexpected inner anguish commensurate with the solemnity of the moment. Her "very heart trembled with shame and sorrow for his unfeeling interruption of their sacred adoration, for all around was dead silence and many were prostrated" (*EBS*, 291). Involuntarily she bowed low in reverence "to the pavement and thought secretly on the word of Saint Paul with starting tears, 'They discern not the Lord's Body'" (*EBS*, 291).

Elizabeth's spontaneous emotional response was a prelude to her understanding of the Eucharist in the Church and in her own life. God was preparing her heart to cherish the privilege of receiving Jesus Christ in the Eucharist. The Spirit stirred deep within her. Next she thought "how should they eat and drink their very damnation for not discerning it, if indeed it is not there. Yet, how should it be there?" (*EBS*, 291). The Holy Spirit had planted the question in her soul. Its percolation would take time.

Elizabeth's encounter with the Real Presence in Montenero drew her toward Roman Catholicism. Her desire for truth enabled her to grapple with questions of faith. The Holy Spirit guided her search during which she responded to grace. Elizabeth's reverence for the Real Presence led her beyond chapel pews into apostolic ministry to the people of God. Elizabeth engaged in various forms of evangelization in her charitable and educational mission. Her unswerving belief in God's loving presence in the Blessed

Sacrament led her to discover the presence of God in needy children and in persons who were lonely, sick, and dying. In the neighbor she encountered her God (see Matthew 25:45). Her example invites us to examine how the Eucharist continues to be the source of nourishment for the people of God.

LIFE OF MY LIFE

Elizabeth never lost her sense of wonder for the mystery of the Eucharist. She left an account of her first Communion: "At last, GOD IS MINE and I AM HIS. Now let all go its round. I HAVE RECEIVED HIM" (*EBS*, 376). Despite her earnest preparations of the evening before, a fearful foreboding arose within her that her efforts were insufficient yet she was also full of "transports of confidence and hope in God's GOODNESS" (*EBS*, 377). Confidence in God's compassionate mercy paved her path to eternity.

Elizabeth's gnawing hunger for the Eucharist was never satisfied. On her deathbed when there was a question of breaking her fast to take a little drink, she denied human comfort to fulfill the longing of her soul. She said simply but firmly that she wanted to receive the Lord one last time. Throughout her life her thanksgivings after Communion were profound and prolonged, giving the impression of mystical union.

Elizabeth's great reverence for the mystery of God in others and the activity of grace in souls made the Eucharist truly the fountainhead of her life. Its reception prompted feelings of consolation and peace in her heart. In one of her meditations Elizabeth outlines the elements of her eucharistic spirituality. Its title, "Preparation, Reception, Thanks, Eternity," describes how she viewed the Eucharist (see *CPR*). Hers was a pathway through a labyrinth of prayer, reflection, and self-knowledge which converged in intimate encounters with her God.

The Spirit led Elizabeth into an ever deepening knowledge of God as her all and the source of her life. She could not imagine one being close to the Divine and consciously choosing a sinful path of separation. At times she was at a loss for words and simply pleaded with her "Friend and Guardian" to "*hear* the Voice of my Love, and of my Misery. *Live always* in me, and let me live perpetually in You, and for You, as I live only by You" (*EBS*, 178; 448). Elizabeth's reflection prompts us to ask ourselves, "What is my life when I do not live in God?"

The Eucharist impelled Elizabeth toward ministry, sustained her during periods of depression and dryness, and restored the light of God's love in her life. She was impressed by the *Anima Christi*, a prayer of Saint Ignatius of Loyola which Elizabeth adapted according to her devotion by adding: "in life, in death—in time and Eternity—in the hour of death defend me, call me to come to you, receive me with your Saints in glory everlasting" (*SW*, 337).

In her version of this prayer Elizabeth begged that the "Soul of Jesus" would sanctify her and that the "Spirit of Jesus" and the "Love of Jesus" would enliven her innermost being (*SW*, 337). From her experiences in Italy until the last of her grace-filled days in Saint Joseph's Valley, Elizabeth's sole desire was union with God. In her words, her "whole Soul desired only him" (*EBS*, 293). She was a person of the Eucharist whose life was a great "Amen" to God's plan for her.

REFLECTION QUESTIONS

Do I believe in the centrality of the Eucharist in my spiritual life? How do I prepare myself to participate in the celebration of the Eucharist? To receive the Eucharist? How do I make a thanksgiving after receiving holy Communion? Do I welcome the Lord? Do I thank him for giving me the opportunity to receive him that day? Do I ask him to preserve me from sin and from a sudden and unprovided death? Do I pray for others? In the spirit of Elizabeth, am I conscious of the relationship between receiving Jesus Christ in the Eucharist and finding Jesus in my neighbors in need?

DAY SEVEN

Religious Conversion: "Light of Truth"

FOCUS POINT

Religious conversion is an outcome of one's desire for God and search for truth. Elizabeth prayed for the gift of faith for her salvation. She underwent a heart-wrenching struggle to discover the Church governed by the successor of the apostle Peter. In making her profession of faith as a Roman Catholic, Elizabeth found inner peace. She lived live her faith with integrity (*LG*, 8).

I assure you my becoming a Catholic was a very simple consequence of going to a Catholic country where it was impossible for anyone interested in any religion not to see the wide difference between the first established Faith given, and founded by our Lord and his Apostles, and the various forms it has since taken. As I had always delighted in reading the Scriptures, I had so deep an impression of the mysteries of Divine revelation that

though full of the sweet thought that every good and well mean-
ing Soul was right, I determined when I came home, both in duty
to my children and my own Soul, to learn all I was capable of
understanding on the subject. If ever a Soul did make a fair in-
quiry, our God knows that mine did. Every day of life more and
more increases my gratitude to him for having made me what I
am (Elizabeth Seton to Ann C. Tilghman, January 1820).

A̶t the beginning of her sojourn in Italy, Elizabeth's impressions about Catholics eventually led her to ask questions,
first out of curiosity then out of sincerity. The Filicchis were well
qualified to respond to her inquiries. On the point of different
religious denominations they told her that "there was only one
true Religion" and that a "right Faith" was required for people
to "be acceptable to God" for eternal salvation (*EBS*, 290).

Elizabeth wondered about the afterlife for non-Catholics.
Elizabeth reported that the Filicchis' reply was clear about "where
people will go who can know the right faith, if they pray for it,
and inquire for it, and yet, do neither" (*EBS*, 290). To this Elizabeth retorted to Filippo Filicchi with her quick wit and laughter:
"Sir, you want me to pray and inquire, and be of your Faith!" He
responded respectfully, "Pray, and inquire. That is all I ask you"
(*EBS*, 290). Thus began a spiritual spiral which plunged Elizabeth
into a maze of discernment. Her search for truth was painful.

MYSTERIES OF DIVINE REVELATION

Elizabeth was not born a saint. She attained holiness by how she
responded day by day to God with steadfast love in the circumstances of her life. Over time she gradually paid more attention to
God until one Sunday she declared that day would be "considered the *Birth day* of the Soul" (*EBS*, 209). Like ourselves her
spiritual journey developed over the years in her various life roles—
daughter, wife, mother, widow, and spiritual leader.

As a widow Elizabeth took up the Filicchis' challenge to pray for enlightenment and to inquire about Roman Catholicism. Although historical details of her baptism are unknown, the story of faith begins with her baptism in the Anglican Communion in the Protestant Episcopal Church of New York. Elizabeth's personal conversion was a process marked by choices she made which yielded key moments of grace for her soul. Among these was her profession of faith in Roman Catholicism.

God blessed Elizabeth from her youth with a natural penchant for communing with the Divine. At age fifteen she rode into the woods on a wagon and "soon found an outlet in a meadow and chestnut tree with several young ones growing around it, found rich moss under it and a warm sun.... The air still, a clear blue vault above—the numberless sounds of spring melody" (*Diary*, 17).

Her young heart was filled with "enthusiastic love of God and admiration of his works." At that time she exclaimed: "God was my Father, my all" (*Diary*, 17). She prayed. She reflected. She sang hymns. She cried and engaged in self-talk about how far God could place her above all the sorrows of family conflicts weighing then on her young heart. After two hours of enjoying this contemplative experience she "laid still to enjoy the Heavenly Peace" that came over her soul. She felt she had grown "ten years in the spiritual life" (*Diary*, 17).

During the years she worshiped in Trinity Episcopal Church on Broadway, Elizabeth began keeping spiritual journals in which she noted inspirational passages which struck her. In this way she identified a pivotal point in her relationship with God—a day of personal conversion. "This blessed day, my soul was first sensibly convinced of the blessing and practicability of an entire surrender of itself and all its faculties to God. It has been the *Lord's day* indeed to me" (*ASJPH* 3:6).

Within a few months Elizabeth made some definite resolutions to promote her spiritual growth in Christlike virtue. "Solemnly in the presence of my Judge, I resolve through his grace, to remember my infirmity and my sin; to keep the door of my lips;

to consider the cause of sorrow for sin in myself and [in] them whose souls are so dear to me as my own; to check and restrain all useless words; to deny myself and exercise that severity that I know is due to my sin; Oh judge myself thereby, trusting through mercy that I shall not be severely judged by my Lord" (*ASJPH* 3:7, 2).

A FAIR INQUIRY

As an aid in her search for truth, the Filicchis initially gave Elizabeth a copy of *The Introduction to a Devout Life* by Francis de Sales (1609) and other books for spiritual reading. Elizabeth also "read the promises given to Saint Peter and the 6th chapter of John every day," then asked God how could she offend him by believing in them literally (*EBS*, 317).

Elizabeth enjoyed her reading on religious topics, but in her inimitable way it was with a flair of jest that she quoted Alexander Pope in her journal for Rebecca: "*If I am right, O teach my heart still in the right to stay, if I am wrong thy grace impart to find the better way*" (*EBS*, 290). At that time Elizabeth, in a great spirit of ecumenism, wryly commented, "not that I can think there is a better way than I know" but then added more thoughtfully, "but every one must be respected in their own" beliefs (*EBS*, 290).

In her faith-filled search for truth, Elizabeth read extensively about Catholic dogmas and practices. In the midst of her research and reflection, she sought the counsel of spiritual advisors to whom she had been recommended. Elizabeth had returned to New York with the "heart" of a Roman Catholic but was soon buffeted by waves of religious bigotry.

Willing to pay a price for fidelity to what she believed to be the truth, Elizabeth was confident in her All and "the truth of his promise which never can fail" (*EBS*, 305). Elizabeth's intense inner struggle was so severe to that she felt it "was destroying" her "mortal life and more than that" her "peace with God" (*EBS*, 305).

Elizabeth was "shocked at the idea of being so far from the

truth" (*EBS*, 315). After much prayer, she concluded "that [the Protestant Episcopal Church] was separated from the Church founded by Our Lord and his Apostles, and its ministers without a regular succession from them" (*EBS*, 315).

Faith for salvation was Elizabeth's only goal—"the earnest desire" of her "Soul" (*EBS*, 315). She sought God and truth expecting to find her peace in the true Church, not in the social status of the Catholic congregation whose members were then considered as the riffraff of society. Astonished and befuddled by objectors, Elizabeth soon wavered and fell into confusion complicated by understandable feelings of depression during her search for the true faith.

Elizabeth's perplexity accelerated as the debate swirled and escalated around her. The stakes were high and the risk great. The outcome could jeopardize her children's welfare. She became the talk of the town. Her children worried about her because their mother was so distraught and tearful. These were months of painful confusion within the formerly tranquil Seton family circle. Finally she "looked straight up to God, and...told him since [she] cannot see the way to please you, whom alone [she] wished to please," everything was indifferent to her until God would show her the way for her to walk (*EBS*, 373). She waited on God.

WELL-MEANING SOUL

During her trial of indecision, Elizabeth centered herself using the following outcry of faith like a mantra, "GOD IS MY GOD" (*EBS*, 373). Finally Elizabeth "abandoned all to God" with "a renewed confidence in the Blessed Virgin whose mild and peaceful love" she felt reproached her "bold excesses" as a reminder to set her heart above with God alone (*EBS*, 374).

Elizabeth had discovered her star (see *EBS*, 372). Her search for truth ended. She chose Roman Catholicism and made her profession of faith March 14, 1805, at Saint Peter's Catholic Church in lower Manhattan. Elizabeth found peace and joy.

Elizabeth knew a depth of happiness which renewed her whole

being when she received Jesus Christ in the Eucharist for the first time. She experienced a real rejuvenation of body and soul. Despite her anxieties about the adequacy of her preparation, Elizabeth was filled with "transports of confidence and hope in his GOODNESS" (*EBS*, 377).

Elizabeth left a written account of her first thoughts after receiving her Savior in holy Communion: "Let God arise. Let his enemies be scattered, for it seemed to me my King had come to take his throne, and instead of the humble tender welcome I had expected to give him, it was but a triumph of joy and gladness that the deliverer was come, and my defense and shield and strength and Salvation made mine for this World and the next" (*EBS*, 377).

Her heart danced with fervor but her more reasonable self realized that she must bear fruit in her new life of faith. Elizabeth likened her Communion at Easter to the divine provision of "refreshing waters for which I thirsted truly" (*EBS*, 377).

It was a "greater Mystery" to Elizabeth how the disbelief of people for whom Jesus Christ had suffered and died could exclude themselves from the Eucharist, "the best of all gifts" (*EBS*, 378).

For her, the "blindness of redeemed souls" was incredulous (*EBS*, 378). Elizabeth approached the sacred Liturgy with "grateful and unspeakable joy and reverence" and adoring "the daily renewed virtue of THAT WORD by which we possess him in our blessed MASS, and Communion," but she added "all that is but Words, since Faith is from God" (*EBS*, 378).

Elizabeth acknowledged that receiving the gift of faith and entering the Catholic Church was one of the greatest graces of her life. Gratitude for the opportunity to live her faith actively was a core value for Elizabeth who gave her daughter Catherine Josephine the following advice when she was at the threshold of independence: "Look well to religion *through your life*, and I repeat to you it has been from the first, as it now *is*, the solid joy and triumph of mine" (*MA*, 4).

REFLECTION QUESTIONS

Do I evangelize and support persons who are considering a religious conversion? What religious truths are the anchors of my faith? How is God inviting me to grow in my spiritual life? In what ways is God bidding me to become more involved in my parish? Is God calling me to full-time ministry in the Church? What's missing in my life now? Why? How is God urging me to live the promises of my baptismal commitment more deeply? How does the sacred Liturgy nourish my life of faith? In the spirit of Elizabeth, how does the Word of God guide me along my daily journey of faith?

DAY EIGHT

The Mother of Jesus: "Refuse Nothing"

FOCUS POINT

The Church draws on the love of the Mother of Jesus as a model of faith and charity (see *LG*, 63). She is a model of discipleship in her generous response to the prompting of the Holy Spirit and her unconditional acceptance of God's plan of salvation and redemption by Jesus. In Mary's maternity, Elizabeth found a prism of faith which reflected God's loving mercy and providential care for the human family.

The other day in a moment of excessive distress...my whole Soul desired only God. A little prayer book of Mrs. Filicchi's was on the table. I opened [it to] a little prayer (the Memorare) *of Saint Bernard to the Blessed Virgin, begging her to be our Mother. I said it to her with such a certainty that God would surely refuse nothing to his Mother, and that she could not help loving and pitying the poor Souls he died for...I felt really I had a Mother which...my foolish heart so often lamented to have lost in early days. From the first remembrance of infancy, I have looked in all the plays of childhood and wildness of youth to the clouds for my Mother. At that moment it seemed as if I had found more than her, even in tenderness and pity of a Mother. So I cried myself to sleep on her heart (Elizabeth Seton, Journal for Rebecca Seton, Entry of February 24, 1804).*

M ary is honored as the Mother of God and Mother of the Redeemer. In this way she is also the Mother of all peoples. Present on Pentecost at the birth of the Church, Mary continues her role in the Church as a mediator and intercessor of grace for all believers.

The young maiden of Nazareth and the tiny widow of Leghorn, both women of courageous faith destined to bear heavy crosses, responded to the call of their God who led them into an unknown future. Both faced their destinies with profound trust despite some apprehension. Little did either woman realize how universally their lowly social status would be transformed for future generations to honor them (see Luke 1:48). Elizabeth's filial devotion to Mary as the Mother of God contributed to the blossoming of her gift of the Catholic faith.

MOTHER OF GOD
In her last instruction Elizabeth explains how Mary is the "Mother of our redemption" and how "we honor her continually" in following Christ. She saw that Jesus and Mary were forever intertwined in the economy of salvation, "JESUS in Mary, Mary in JESUS in our prayers" (SW, 329). Focusing on one led Elizabeth to the other. For Elizabeth her discipleship seemed to unfold like a rose bud in relationship to both Mother and Son.

Elizabeth was a person deprived of maternal nurturing in her girlhood and who longed for it over the years especially when feeling vulnerable. Her experience of strong emotional currents at times of loss tended to surface waves of old feelings. "Begging her [Mary] to be our Mother," Elizabeth, as a recent widow, unburdened her soul to Mary in a moment of prayer, and was filled with a deep sense of inner certitude that her supplications would be heard (*EBS*, 293).

Mary's maternity touched Elizabeth to the core. After visiting a Marian shrine in Italy, Elizabeth recorded this reflection: "I am a *Mother* so the Mother's thought came. Also how was my GOD a little babe in the first stage of his mortal existence *in Mary*, but I lost these thoughts in my babes at home, which I daily long for more and more" (*EBS*, 291). Since Mary was the mother of Jesus, the bereaved Elizabeth intuitively felt her maternal solicitude for her newly found celestial friend. That thought drew Elizabeth into deeper relationship with Mary who was "always, everywhere, in every moment, day and night, conscious [that] she was His Mother" (*NC*, 168).

During Elizabeth's stay in Italy, she visited Florence with the Filicchi family. At the Church of *Santa Maria Novella*, Elizabeth was mesmerized by the life-size painting of the *Descent From the Cross*, which engaged her "*whole soul*" and her maternal identification with Mary as a grief-stricken mother permeated to the core of her being. She understood the acute pain of loss which Mary must have felt at her son's crucifixion.

Mary's expression at the foot of the cross seemed to convey that "the iron had entered into her—and the shades of death over her agonized countenance so strongly contrasted the heavenly Peace of the dear Redeemer's that it seems as if his pains had fallen on her"(*CW*, 287). The image kept recurring before her mind's eye. Like Mary, Elizabeth "kept all these things, reflecting on them in her heart" (Luke 2:19). Their pondering was a profound prayer of remembrance.

Elizabeth felt a closeness to Mary. Elizabeth expressed her Marian devotion by honoring Mary in prayer and imitating her virtues. Mary continues to invite us into friendship with her as disciples of Jesus—disciples who have our own personal prayer of remembrance to ponder deep within our hearts.

REMEMBER, O MARY

The prayer of the *Memorare*, composed by Saint Bernard of Clairvaux, earned a pivotal place among Elizabeth's most cherished remembrances. She found comfort in praying to Mary in time of need because "if she is not heard, who shall be?" (*SW*, 56). The Spirit led Elizabeth to understand "Jesus delighted to receive our love embellished and purified through the heart of Mary, as from the heart of a *FRIEND*" (*SW*, 328). For Elizabeth the question of focus was central. She wondered, "how can we honor the mysteries of our Jesus without honoring Mary in them all?" (*SW*, 328).

Elizabeth felt a special bond of maternity with Mary, the Mother of God. Elizabeth often slept with a small crucifix under her pillow and with the Blessed Virgin's picture close to her heart. This personal gesture shows how much Mary's divine motherhood touched and moved her own maternal heart. The motherhood of Mary aroused strong feelings in Elizabeth which drew her into prayerful reflection contemplating the Incarnation, the mystery of Jesus Christ being God and man.

So often grieved by separation and loss, Elizabeth forged a strong spiritual bond with Mary which included a reflection on her experience as an expectant mother. "We honor Mary continually with Our Jesus...his nine months within her...what passed between them...she alone knowing Him—He her only tabernacle—*Mary, full of Grace, Mother of Jesus*" (*SW*, 328). Elizabeth also pondered what it was like for Mary to be the mother of the Savior, thinking of "the Infancy of Jesus—in her lap—on her knees...caressing, playing in her arms" (*NC*, 168).

Realizing how rapidly children grow up and how difficult the separation can be for mothers, Elizabeth reflected on her feeding of the divine infant: "Jesus on the breast of Mary feeding...how long she must have delayed the weaning of such a Child!!!!" (*NC*,

168). What memories the scene must have evoked for Elizabeth who had taken such delight in nursing and caring for her own five children during their infancy.

In Mary, Elizabeth found a window of faith through which she discovered deeper insights of God's love for her. This relationship drew Elizabeth into discovering a wellspring of grace through a bonding of maternal hearts. Her Marian devotion had its genesis in finding the twelfth-century prayer, the *Memorare*, which brought her much consolation and peace. When Elizabeth had finished writing her version of the *Memorare*, she added this poignant phrase: "Love me, my Mother!" (*ASJPH* 19:2e).

The *Memorare* confidently implores the intercession of the Virgin Mary for the needs of the petitioner. In praying to Mary, Elizabeth believed she was turning to a woman whom she saw as a kindred spirit and to whom she turned with confidence for relief, "confiding" in her "goodness and mercy." When offering this prayer Elizabeth begged the "Mother of the *Eternal Word*" to adopt her as her child and "take upon yourself the care of my eternal Salvation" (*ASJPH* 19:2e).

Elizabeth, who had experienced so much disconnection in her earlier life, truly felt she had discovered a maternal figure who would nurture and care for her. Elizabeth felt that she had found more than her own mother could ever have been to her.

ON HER HEART

Elizabeth experienced consolation in Marian devotion. At her confirmation she "added the Name of *Mary* to the *Ann* [and] *Elizabeth*" because to her the names represented "the three most endearing ideas in the World" encompassing "the moments of the Mysteries of Salvation" (*EBS*, 408). The trio of mothers connected the new convert to the mothers of Jesus, Mary, and John the Baptist. Each instrument of God in the plan of salvation represented a way of discipleship that attracted Elizabeth—Jesus, the obedient Servant; Mary, the handmaid of the Lord; and John, the precursor of the Messiah.

Over time Elizabeth came to a deeper understanding of the role of Mary in the Church and what it meant to be a Catholic woman of faith. "The glory and happiness of the Catholic Church is to sing the praises of Mary. The striking proof she is the true spouse of Christ since she best loves, honors, and cherishes her whom Jesus Christ himself so much honors, loves, and cherishes" (*NC*, 167). Elizabeth could relate to Mary as a woman. She believed she could count on her and knew that God would hear the pleas of his Mother and surely not refuse anything to her.

Elizabeth saw Mary as a model and teacher in the spiritual life, particularly in her unconditional "Yes" to the angel Gabriel who announced the good news of the Incarnation (see Luke 1:19). Mary stood out for Elizabeth as an icon or model of grace for believers to imitate. Mary, no doubt, also became Elizabeth's confidant in the transition of her life roles from being "Widow Seton" to "Mother Seton" and all that change cost her.

Mary shines like a beacon of grace in her feminine resilience as a courageous woman of faith. Elizabeth often reveled about "[t]he glory and happiness of Mary—her predestination—was loved with an eternal love. What then the delight of the Holy Trinity in her! (…) Her obscure life: humble, poor, retired, modest, a model to young virgins—gloriously hidden in God" (*NC*, 167).

Elizabeth expressed her Marian devotion, not only in the celebration of the liturgical feasts honoring Mary, but also by writing inspirational journal entries, instructions, and special meditations. Elizabeth's passion for seeking God's will often moved her to encourage her religious daughters to greater spiritual vitality, challenging them to be women of prayer and to do everything possible by way of formation and preparation to do justice to their vocation. She also reminded them that Mary was "the first Sister of Charity on earth" (*SW*, 329).

Elizabeth owned a large oil painting of Our Lady of Guadalupe, which hung in the small chapel at Emmitsburg where she spent time in daily prayer. Elizabeth entrusted her special intentions to Mary and often commended her sons, William and

Richard, to the care of Mary, Star of the Ocean, while they were at sea. Elizabeth also asked Mary, Queen of Apostles, to intercede for the needs of the clergy, specifically for her dear friend and confidant at Mount Saint Mary's, Simon Gabriel Bruté. Like Elizabeth we look to Mary for strength in living the commitments which we made by our personal *"Yes"* to grow in Divine Love and to be the compassion of Christ to persons in need.

THE MEMORARE OF ELIZABETH SETON

Remember, O most pious Virgin Mary,
that no one ever had recourse to you,
implored your help or sought your mediation,
without obtaining relief.
Confiding then on your goodness and mercy,
I cast myself at your sacred feet,
and do most humbly supplicate you,
O, Mother of the Eternal Word,
to adopt me as your child and take upon yourself
the care of my eternal Salvation.
O, let it not be said, my dearest Mother,
that I have perished, where no one ever found but grace
and Eternal Salvation.
Love me, my Mother! (ASJPH 19:2e).

REFLECTION QUESTIONS

Do I turn to Mary, Mother of Jesus, as an intercessor or mediatrix of grace in my life? How do I respond to such moments of divine inspiration? What difference does that make in my personal relationship to God? To my neighbor? To myself? How is Mary's *"Yes"* a model for my growth in the spiritual life? How does God ask me to say *"Yes"* in my life? What are some of the moments of grace in my life that I wish to ponder in my heart for further reflection and prayer? In the spirit of Elizabeth, in what ways does Mary draw me closer to her son Jesus?

DAY NINE

Faith in God: "Redeeming Love"

FOCUS POINT

Eternal life begins with faith in God. For this gift to thrive through-out life, it must be nourished with the Word of God. We also must ask God to increase our faith so that it may deepen and enable us to live it more fully like Elizabeth who was fed by the Word of God and the Bread of Life. She grew spiritually and manifested a special concern for her neighbor in need.

Received the Longing Desire of my soul. Merciful Lord, what a Privilege! And my dearest Anna, too. The bonds of Nature and Grace all twined together. The Parent offers the Child, the Child the Parent, and both are united in the Source of their Being—and rest together on Redeeming Love. May we never, never leave the sheltering wing, but dwelling now under the shadow of His Cross, we will cheerfully gather the thorns which will be turned hereaf-ter into a joyful crown (Elizabeth Seton, Spiritual Journal for Cecilia Seton, Entry of August 23, 1807).

The revelation of divine love is the gift of faith God gives to the human family (see Hebrews 11:1). Although faith is first received as a supernatural virtue at baptism, one needs the ongoing assistance of the Holy Spirit. Contemplating the blessings of this gift on earth is like gazing at a reflection in a mirror. Through the image we may perceive the wonderful things of God for faith-filled persons who live their lives radically rooted in gospel values.

Elizabeth's belief that divine promises would be fulfilled fueled the sacred fire of love within her soul. Like her, we are called to walk by faith, not by sight, on our pilgrimage on earth (see 2 Corinthians 5:7). We are called to be witnesses of faith by living gospel values on the job, in the marketplace, and at home. Despite passing shadows and darkness, we like Elizabeth before us, are called to transform the love of God in our hearts into concrete forms of service for the least of our brothers and sisters (see Matthew 25:31–46). This is the legacy of charity and justice of Elizabeth who fixed her eyes on Jesus, "the leader and perfecter of faith" (see Hebrews 12:1–2).

LONGING DESIRE

Having placed her belief securely in God, Elizabeth trusted that her Loving Parent would provide for her. This was her firm conviction from her youth. After a day when Elizabeth had experienced divine favor abundantly, she wrote reflectively: "This day I trust is noted for me in the Book of Life. Oh, that the blessings received, and the glorious privileges I have enjoyed in it, may be the incitement to faithful discharge through divine Grace of every duty which my dear and gracious Master may give me to perform; that it may make me his own in thought, word, and deed forever, leading me to the Supreme Good—the blessing of losing myself and all things in Him" (SW, 87).

Elizabeth expressed her yearning for God in various ways as she matured. In adulthood as she tried to live a devout life more conscientiously, she realized that the work of God prospers better with human cooperation. Elizabeth, like ourselves, lent her eyes, hands, and heart to accomplishing the work of God among the human family. In so doing Elizabeth understood that God was using life circumstances to bring her soul into deeper relationship with the Holy Trinity. This immersion into divine love engaged Elizabeth's whole being.

At the same time, however, conscious of her human limitations, Elizabeth sometimes asked herself if she realized the presence and magnitude of God in her life. She marveled about "the protecting presence [and] *the consoling grace of my Redeemer and God*" (*SW*, 89). The mutuality of her relationship with God bespeaks her closeness to the divine Lover. She felt protected and consoled by the action of God in her life.

Her familiarity with the psalms was as an integral expression of her life of faith deeply rooted in God's love. As such Elizabeth could allude to them in her writings The following example in which she refers to psalms 113 and 91 illustrates how Elizabeth perceived herself in God's tender care. "He raises me from the dust to feel that I am near Him. He drives away all terrors to fill me with his consolations. He is my *Guide*, my *Friend*, and *Supporter*. With such a Guide, can I fear? With such a Friend, shall I not be *satisfied*? With such a Supporter, can I fall?" (*SW*, 89).

Like all of us Elizabeth understood that doing God's will sometimes involves human cost but she was willing to pay the price. Her prayer was that she would obey God generously, not reluctantly. "Lord, here am I, the creature of your will" (*SW*, 89). Elizabeth rejoiced in the lead of God who was her divine Shepherd. As a Christian she was filled with gratitude for having been chosen for discipleship despite feelings of inadequacy and unworthiness. She was thankful for the gift of faith she had received and expressed her deepest desire to God. "Only continue to [give] me thy Soul-cheering presence. In Life, or in Death, let me be your own" (*SW*, 89). God invites us to do the same.

SHELTERING WING

Elizabeth trusted God as a loving parent whose sheltering wing provided protection. In pondering the story of John, the disciple whom Jesus loved and who had reclined on his chest during the Last Supper, Elizabeth inverted the relationship suggesting that indeed we do not rest on his breast but he on ours since "our life in him [is] wrapped in him" (*SW*, 330; see also John 21:20). Indeed Elizabeth saw her life enclosed with Jesus Christ. He was her All. Enfolded with Jesus, Elizabeth felt secure. She knew she could trust the God of Promise and rely on the divine Word.

Elizabeth wrote a reflection in which she described an insight that the names of the disciples of Jesus and the good shepherds were recorded for all eternity. Their remembrance remains alive in the eucharistic Presence of the Blessed Sacrament, "now from his tabernacle here—to our very heart!" (*SW*, 330). The memory of God's goodness to the human family took root in Elizabeth's heart and inspired her to be a woman whose love gave witness to the gospel throughout her life.

At times Elizabeth, like ourselves, felt inner turmoil and the need of healing and reconciliation. She turned to the "Spirit of God" begging for the grace to "fix the wavering mind, constrain the wayward *will*, [and] subdue the powers of disobedience"(*SW*, 91). She prayed for herself when circumstances diminished her sense of control and her nerves were frayed. The ardor of her faith prompted her to wish that her savior and redeemer would "bring each Soul to its center of blessedness" (*SW*, 91). The essence of this prayer guided her life and her actions. Elizabeth was driven by a desire to share her religious ardor with others.

Elizabeth wrote "First Communion Instructions" for the children who would receive the Eucharist for the first time. Emphasizing that they were about to receive the body and blood of Christ, she presented this privilege as a sacred opportunity to begin their "dear union here with God" which she hoped they would "carry on so happily through *Life, Death, and Eternity*" (*FCI*, 1).

The redeeming love of her savior had not only been a sheltering wing, but also the fountain of eternal love in her life. Her grateful heart realized God's choice of her and her understanding of this grace grew throughout her life. "My JESUS first called me from *nothing, drew me* in pity *to him, loved me* first with an Eternal Love, and then called me to *love him*, and gave himself *for me*...bled and died *for me* upon *the cross*, after being a little Infant *for me* in the manger" (*FCI*, 2).

Elizabeth tried to convey the tenderness of God's love for each person by sending his son as the Redeemer. Since most of her pupils were young children, she explained that divine love is "more than a Mother's love" (*FCI*, 3). When preparing for holy Communion Elizabeth exhorted them to bear in mind the following sentiments: "Oh my Jesus, it is your love and mercy which calls me to You, let then that same love and mercy prepare me for You" (*FCI*, 3). God's love and mercy continues to invite us to this same wonderful sacrament of love.

JOYFUL CROWN

God's love permeated Elizabeth's being with grace and led her ultimately to eternal glory in the beatific vision. Simon Gabriel Bruté was Elizabeth's friend, confessor, and spiritual director for almost ten years. At the end of her life he was convinced of her holiness. Bruté held the opinion that it was not possible "to find similar or great elevation, purity, and love of God, heaven, or supernatural and eternal things than were found in her" (*MS*, 299).

As Elizabeth's personal experience of the Spirit intensified, so too did her understanding of human relationships. She was keenly aware of the everlasting dimensions of being a sole parent. Her children's eternal salvation was a lifelong preoccupation which she continually brought to prayer. She hoped for a grand family reunion in heaven.

Elizabeth seems to have been naturally contemplative and given to resting in God as a preferred prayer form. She advised that prayer be "literally without ceasing—without ceasing, in every occurrence and employment of our lives" (*EBS*, 389). This was a key to her sanctity and the efficacy of her mission of charity. She advocated "prayer of the heart" as continual attentiveness to the Spirit at the core of one's being. This heartfelt communion of love Elizabeth described as being "independent of place or situation, or which is rather a habit of lifting up the heart to God, as in a constant communication with Him" (*EBS*, 389).

When referring to God in her journals and correspondence, Elizabeth used numerous names which revealed her many images of the Divine. Among these are the following: Blessed Savior, Blessed Spirit, Father of All, Father of all Mercies, Friend, God Almighty, Guardian, Omnipotent Jesus, Jesus Babe, Redeemer, and Spirit of Peace and Patience. This variety reveals the complexity yet profound simplicity of her relationship with her Creator.

She spent time conversing with God in daily prayer. The ties that bound Elizabeth to this earth dissolved in the face of the allurement of divine love. She expressed her sentiments ardently in "A Prayer to Jesus" whom she addressed as "My Dear, my Amiable JESUS" *(SW,* 332). In the text of this prayer Elizabeth turns to her "tender Redeemer" and "My Merciful Lord" from whom she sought assistance in times of distress.

Elizabeth makes her petition in these words: "My faith, My Hope, and my desires are fixed on You alone" *(SW,* 332). Jesus was her All—the focus of her life. Elizabeth pleads with her savior for what she seeks: "O *JESUS,* sure joy of my soul, give me but a true love of You. Let me seek You as my only good" (*SW,* 332).

Elizabeth's path to God was unique. It was her own personal pathway of holiness as a wife, mother, and widow devoted to the gospel. She lived her life simply, guided by this principle: "Leave all to Him, all you have to do is *Pray, Pray*" (*EBS,* 539). Her spiritual journey could be summarized as follows: "Faith lifts the staggering soul on one side. Hope supports it on the other. Experience says it must be—and love says let it be" (March 26, 1810). Elizabeth's advice to us would be the same.

REFLECTION QUESTIONS

Do I live my faith in God with integrity? Who is God for me? How do I address God in prayer? What is my favorite name for God? When do I most experience God's love for me? Do I feel I can trust God? Why? If not, do I feel free to express my fears to God? How would I describe my personal pathway to God? What are some of the opportunities I have now to grow in God's love? What challenges must I deal with to be more Christlike? In the spirit of Elizabeth, in what ways does God continue to be a source of redeeming love in my life?

DAY TEN

Confiding Friendship: "Tell Me Your Heart"

FOCUS POINT

The gift of friendship is one of life's priceless treasures (see Sirach 6:5–17). Deep bonds of affection and esteem united Elizabeth with her friends in mutuality and reciprocity. The simplicity and availability with which Elizabeth gave of her deepest self in friendship was one of her most outstanding characteristics. She models authentic listening to self, the other, and God.

My dearest Friend,
Pain and sorrow are our constant companions, my dear friend, and where can we look for rest but in Eternity? (…) You will ever love us, my own friend. While away from all to whom we are allied by natural affection, aliens to our nearest connections and seeking bread among strangers, my soul cries after you as its dearest Sister and rests assured of your love. Yes, we are among strang-

ers in one sense of the word—but not strangers in kindness nor affection. For we never received so much before since we were left desolate but from you. Madame [Françoise-Victoire] Fournier, the sister of our Superior [William Dubourg], assists me in all the little cares for my children, [in Baltimore] if there is a finger ache she watches over us. Mrs. [Robert] Barry and her husband omit nothing that generosity or kindness can dictate. I do not fear that they will be wearied in their attentions because I know the principle on which they act...and will you not write your own friend and tell me your heart—do, do my Dué write close and small, many is the long day since I have heard from you—dear, dear, dear friend, farewell! Ever your own friend, MEAS (Elizabeth Seton to Catherine (Dué) Dupleix, June 20, 1808).

The life-giving qualities of openness, trust, and communication characterize the true friendships Jesus had with his disciples—"I have called you friends, because I have told you everything I have heard from my Father" (John 15:15). Elizabeth had a Christlike attitude of welcome and inclusiveness for the kingdom with her extensive network of friends.

Elizabeth enjoyed the blessing of true friendship throughout her life and expressed her sentiments on the subject: "The longer I live and more I reflect and know how to value the realities of Friendship, the more precious that distinction becomes and I look forward to the dear hope that my Sweet Child will also enjoy it" (*EBS*, 10). Elizabeth enjoyed deeply spiritual friendships with her closest lifelong friends. She also guided others as a friend and mentor and was a sturdy shelter for them in their joys and sorrows. The charm of Elizabeth attracted friends.

TENDERNESS OF HEART
Elizabeth's personal relationships usually included some threads of spirituality. She and her friends moved together to God. Among

her innermost circle of friends from New York were three women whose enduring friendships survived the test of time.

Elizabeth corresponded with Julia Sitgreaves Scott for over twenty years. Julia was her confidant and a steadfast support come what may. "You surely know that your steady, unremitting affection in my worldly shipwreck is a sweet consolation, and one of the very few remaining endearments of this life" (*EBS*, 418).

In her letters Elizabeth always gave a motherly account of "her darlings" and inquired after Julia's son and daughter. When Julia became the grandmother of twins, Elizabeth commented insightfully: "I think had it pleased God I could have been a Grandmother, I would have been more tied to this life by a second generation than a first" (October 5, 1817).

Julia was also a generous and constant benefactor whose beneficence provided not only dancing lessons for Anna Maria, medical care for Rebecca when she was lame from a tubercular tumor, outfits for Elizabeth's sons, but also the offer of a home for Catherine Josephine. In one of her last letters, Elizabeth told Julia that she had received her "letter of such love and unexampled friendship, that after reading it with tears over and over, it is deposited with the little sacred memorials of times past which we can only part with in Death" (January 12, 1819).

Elizabeth punctuated her friendships with spirituality because she wanted the best for those whom she loved, particularly with Julia for whom she wished "an Eternity of happy years to my Julia, where only you can know, how dearly you are loved by your *EA Seton*" (January 12, 1819).

Elizabeth told her cherished friend, Eliza Craig Sadler, that "there is not an hour of my Life in which I do not either want the advice or soothing of Friendship" (*EBS*, 18). Elizabeth wished to share her joy at the beauty of Saint Joseph's Valley, and wrote gleefully to her friend, "my heart feels as bright as the Sun now setting and wants to share with you" (May 27, 1810).

Another devoted friend, Catherine Mann Dupleix, affectionately called "Dué," was a non-Catholic from Ireland, but she became a Catholic after Elizabeth went to Emmitsburg. To her Elizabeth wrote, "our Adored gave us a heart to love each other without restraints, calculations, or fears of saying too much or too little" (February 4, 1811). Such mutual friendships supported Elizabeth throughout her life and sustained her in her many vocational roles.

STRAIGHT IN THE PATH

Her sister-in-law Rebecca Seton and Simon Gabriel Bruté stand out among Elizabeth's friends with whom she shared deep spiritual bonds. Mutuality prevailed; both parties were givers and receivers. They supported one another in their relationship with God. These spiritual friendships reflect Elizabeth's efforts to live gospel values and to grow in virtue through true friendship.

Rebecca was six years younger than Elizabeth, but together they inspired one another in religious fervor and devotion. The two sisters-in-law considered one another as "soul sisters" and their kindred spirits fired one another's zeal for love of God and neighbor. Elizabeth frequently jotted notes to Rebecca that revealed the flames of love rising from within her soul.

The following comment from one of her notes probably refers to a stirring sermon preached by an Episcopalian priest whom they both admired: "'My cup has indeed run over' my darling Soul's Sister. Never would I have thought of such enjoyment in *this world*. Last night was surely a *foretaste* of the next, nor *pain* nor *weight*, either of Soul or Body" (*EBS*, 208). In hopes that William Magee might be influenced to attend church services with them, Elizabeth noticed him doing devotional reading and shared her joy with Rebecca. "Since a *quarter* before three I have been, O how happy! Come, come 'Soul's Sister,' *let us Bless the day together one Body, one Spirit, one hope, one God. The Father of All*" (*EBS*, 232).

In departing for Italy with her husband and daughter, Elizabeth reassured Rebecca that the Setons' destiny was in God's hands. Focused heavenward, Elizabeth wrote: "I neither look behind nor before *only up*, there is my rest, and I want nothing" (*EBS*, 244).

On her sad return to the United States the next year, Elizabeth was grieved to learn that her "soul sister" was dying of tuberculosis. She lamented the passing of "the Society of Sisters united by prayer and divine affections, the evening hymns, the daily lectures [spiritual reading], the sunset contemplations, the service of holy days, the Kiss of Peace, the widows visits" and plaintively wrote "all—all—gone forever. Is Poverty and Sorrow the only exchange [for] my husband, my sisters, my home, my comforts?" (*EBS*, 308).

Simon Gabriel Bruté and Elizabeth were kindred spirits whose souls were filled with the same ardor. They mutually enriched and supported one another along their paths to God. Elizabeth helped Bruté learn English and he facilitated her road to sanctity. Elizabeth also counseled Bruté in his spiritual growth. To him Elizabeth revealed a characteristic of her approach to God: "I see God himself in silence and love *through all* [circumstances]" (Christmastide 1818). Earlier when reflecting on her own call to establish the Sisters of Charity, Elizabeth had written: "I set out a new career—Peace and Silence and submission the whole aim" (*ASJPH* 12:32). In living out her vocation Elizabeth asked herself every day "what I do for it in my little part assigned, and can see nothing but to smile, caress, be patient, write, pray and WAIT before him [God]" (*ASJPH* 12:66).

PATH OF VIRTUE AND INTEGRITY

Concerned for the spiritual well-being of her youngest sister-in-law Cecilia Seton, Elizabeth shared her most ardent desire for this child. "May God make you his Own is the prayer of my Soul" (*EBS*, 390). When Cecilia converted to Roman Catholicism at age fifteen, the Setons falsely accused Elizabeth of proselytization. Elizabeth, who also suffered from ostracization of former supporters, simply reminded Cecilia that "Sis has her ups and downs as well as you" (*EBS*, 526).

Elizabeth continued to counsel Cecilia to read the *Imitation of Christ* by Thomas á Kempis and to "be confident in Jesus. Do not suffer yourself to dwell on the changes and variations of your own dear heart while you simply feel it is *His*. Do not mind any other disposition, his most favored Servants are most subject to these imperfections which are an accompaniment of the struggles of Nature and Grace. He, who conquered for us, has his sheltering wing now over my darling" (*EBS*, 527). Cecilia later came to Emmitsburg and joined the Sisters of Charity.

Elizabeth developed another deeply spiritual friendship with Cecilia Maria O'Conway of Philadelphia, who was the first candidate to join Elizabeth in Baltimore, and, therefore, the first Sister of Charity in North America. Known as Sister Cecilia (or Veronica), Elizabeth also affectionately called her "Vero" or "Cis." Initially Sister Cecilia taught at Saint Joseph's Academy (Emmitsburg) but in 1817 went on mission to begin the Roman Catholic Orphan Asylum in New York City.

Elizabeth knew Sister Cecilia's personal struggles and uncertainties and wisely guided the younger woman in her quest for God. Elizabeth wrote Sister Cecilia not to lose sight of the eternal consequence of her actions and encouraged her to go forth in faith to meet her grace regardless of personal reluctance because God had abundant graces to give for her generous response (see *SW*, 303).

Sister Cecilia's heart was drawn more toward a contemplative lifestyle in the cloister than the active apostolate. Elizabeth challenged Cecilia to recognize the needs of the Church in America for self-sacrificing disciples in roles of direct service. In an almost passionate outcry of loving, maternal solicitude, Elizabeth tenderly expressed her fondest wish for this sister of whom she was especially fond: "My Celia, child of my Soul, to OUR GOD, I commit you" (*SW*, 298). Two years after Elizabeth's death, Sister Cecilia transferred to the Ursulines in Montreal and was known as Mother Marie of the Incarnation.

Growth and asceticism, happiness and heartache were integral parts of the spiritual journey Elizabeth shared with others. Rooted in trust, each person felt free to challenge the other to greater love of God and others. We each face that same challenge in our own call to grow in holiness day by day.

REFLECTION QUESTIONS

Do my friendships bring me closer to God? Reflect God's love? Support me in prayer? Challenge me to grow spiritually? How do my friends encourage me to become more Christlike? Do I allow myself to befriend people in need? To guide them on their spiritual journey? To receive insights from them? In what ways do I mentor or guide others along their path to God? How open am I to the surprises of the Holy Spirit in these relationships? In what ways do I go forth in faith to embrace new opportunities? In the spirit of Elizabeth, do I place all my trust in God?

DAY ELEVEN

Living the Paschal Mystery: "Communion of the Cross"

FOCUS POINT

All persons are called to live the Paschal Mystery of the suffering, death, and resurrection of Jesus Christ (see Philippians 2:5–11). Believers celebrate this mystery in Word and sacrament (see *LG*, §3). At the core of the Good News of salvation is Christ's cross and resurrection which accomplished God's saving plan for humankind. Elizabeth realized the importance of bearing the cross of Christ in her life.

There is no possible advantage to be compared with the happiness of receiving Our Lord and Savior in the Holy Eucharist, who is our very life in all our sufferings yet we also receive Him by the communion of His cross.... We may unite with Him, we draw His Spirit on us, and it is very certain that we receive no grace in the communion of the Holy Eucharist but in proportion as we receive it in the communion of the cross.... In receiving his cross we are not to look at what it is made of, that is, on the nature of our sufferings, it being a mystery. We are to look only at the interior virtue, not the exterior form. Eternal life is hidden under it, and when it comes in the shape of poverty, it conceals eternal treasures; in that of shame or reproach it is the glory of God; the form of its afflictions carries eternal consolations. When our Savior offers us his cross in any way, it is Himself (Elizabeth Seton, Meditation on the Communion of the Cross, 52).

E lizabeth viewed the many crosses in her life in light of the salvific cross of Jesus Christ. Her faith enabled her to personally know God as her redeemer, who brought her into the unending circle of divine love. She understood and took personally the promise of Jesus, "when I am lifted up from the earth, I will draw everyone to myself" (John 12:32). In her life Elizabeth gave clear witness that God was drawing her into an ever deeper relationship with her loving savior.

For Elizabeth, her eternal reward depended upon her successful passage through the school of the cross during her earthly life. She focused on union with Jesus as the "suffering servant" of God. For her, the cross was a portal for divine life. Despite feeling overwhelmed at times from deprivation, suffering, illness, and death, Elizabeth focused her eyes on the gaze of Jesus and reciprocated his love. Elizabeth truly believed that all things were possible with God and looked to God alone in all events and circumstances of her life (see Matthew 19:26).

OUR VERY LIFE

The cross of Christ was central in Elizabeth's life. Living it was her objective. Union with her savior was her goal, which she attained by living the Paschal Mystery day by day. For Elizabeth it was incomprehensible that any other plan could make reparation to God or reconcile the human family with her loving Creator except by way of the suffering, dying, and rising of Jesus Christ.

A dominant strain in the melody of Elizabeth's life was her conviction of God's abiding presence in every situation, whether it yielded adversity or prosperity. Despite incredible tragedy and even in the midst of excruciating emotional trials, Elizabeth was able to draw courage from her wellspring of inner resources. On one such occasion, at the beginning of the Setons' thirty days of quarantine in the lazaretto, Elizabeth expressed the following sentiments in a spirit of fervent hope: "If sufferings abound in us, God's consolations also greatly abound, and far exceed all utterance" (*EBS*, 253).

Elizabeth approached life as a person content with her situation because her faith in God prepared her for whatever she might encounter. Her spirit was tuned to God. Her attitude was positive as she accustomed herself to accept the cross in various sizes and shapes.

Even when sailing to Italy Elizabeth had her treasures with her—her religious books and notes, which provided some relief to her aching heart. Her dispositions regarding her suffering invite our imitation. "[I was] not only willing to take [up] my *cross* but kissed it too" (*EBS*, 257). "My Heart is lifted, feels *its treasure*. The little cabin and my cross are objects of peace and sweet comfort. God is with me and what can I fear?" (*EBS*, 225).

Her personal experiences in living the rhythm of the Paschal Mystery in her life enabled her to give wise counsel to others in times of trial. Knowing that a resurrection follows death, Elizabeth offered the following advice to George Weis, a friend in Baltimore: "Blessed a thousand, thousand times be the One who governs all, and will bring light out of darkness" (June 24, 1811). When providing reassurance to Catherine Mann Dupleix, Elizabeth reminded this New York friend that "*Our God loves US*— that is our comfort. We have every true consolation and must leave all to him" (January 1816). Elizabeth's ability to abandon affairs to God freed her from anxiety and fretful worry.

Elizabeth describes her efforts at abandonment in this way: "I gave myself up to God and prayer, encouraging myself with the hope that my unrighteousness would be no more remembered at the foot of the Cross, and that sincere and unremitted asking would be answered in God's own time" (*EBS*, 341). God's answer drew Elizabeth into wholeness and holiness.

INTERIOR VIRTUE

Human weakness and the pain of interpersonal conflict shaped Elizabeth's character and occasioned numerous encounters with the cross. Elizabeth's life was like a beach awaiting the refreshing touch of ocean tides. Her openness to the epiphanies of the mystery of God made her receptive to the divine plan as it unfolded in surprising ways. Elizabeth saw that God often directed her destiny with human instruments.

Frequent reception of the Eucharist was not the norm and it was customary to receive holy Communion according to the permission of a spiritual director or religious superior during Elizabeth's lifetime. With that in mind Elizabeth wrote the following meditation on the relationship of the Paschal Mystery to the Eucharist: "The great advantage of the communion of the cross is, that we receive it when *Our Lord* himself pleases, and at the time He sees best. The ministers of his altar may be mistaken in sending us to communion. They may easily be deceived by us, since we so easily *deceive ourselves*. Through self love, we may go to the Table of our Lord when he did not call us there, when he only bears with our presence, but we never receive him in the communion of the cross without being called by Himself. It is a mandate from heaven itself we obey" (*CC*, 53).

Ever attentive to the voice of the Spirit in her life, Elizabeth developed deeper insight into the meaning of discipleship for herself. In reflecting on the role of the cross, she concluded that, like Saint Paul the apostle, in weakness there is strength (see 2 Corinthians 12:9–10). Elizabeth saw the paschal dimension to her life as a source to be mined through prayer and virtuous living: "We are never strong enough to bear our cross, it is the cross which carries us, nor so weak to be unable to bear it, since the weakest become strong by its virtue" (CC, 58).

Elizabeth knew the pain incurred in the crucible of suffering but realized the necessity of this process of purification. By carrying so many heavy crosses of personal loss, financial ruin, illness, death, and the alienation of family and friends, Elizabeth grew in virtue and God's grace. Indeed, suffering generated hope in her soul. In her journal, "Dear Remembrances," Elizabeth expressed how satisfied she felt after having coped with "the thousand encounters of the CROSS" which she had "embraced so cordially" (SW, 350).

At Emmitsburg Elizabeth found herself faced with managing a conflict which had to be handled with great prudence. Elizabeth wrote directly to Archbishop John Carroll explaining that if the matter involved only her "own happiness" she would "say how good is the cross for me. This is my opportunity to ground myself in patience and perseverance." Since the matter involved the Sisters of Charity, she could not suffer in silence but must be their advocate (SW, 267).

Elizabeth sought to be a person of peace and propriety. She avoided creating friction or doing harm, trying valiantly to control her fiery temper. "Not in any instance or by any provocation to retaliate anger or passion—to speak harshly or severely, *even if the truth*, of any fellow creature, in all difficulties and situations contrary to the bent of my inclination *to remember my cross* and for what purpose I wear it—in the name of my Savior and in firm reliance and trust in *His* assistance" (ASJPH 18:63).

ETERNAL CONSOLATIONS

Elizabeth accepted her crosses and came to know both herself and her God better through suffering. She recognized that she received grace through her crosses. Elizabeth epitomizes the paradoxical side of life. In her vulnerability she had courageous strength, in her poverty she discovered the pearl of great price (see Matthew 13:46). Elizabeth saw her redeemer as the source of vitality for her life.

Through faith Elizabeth came to a more profound understanding of the meaning of the redemption for herself (see 1 John 4:10; Romans 5:8). She steadfastly focused on her eternal goal. "Poverty and sorrow! Well, with God's blessing you too shall be changed into dearest friends. To the world you show your outward garments but through them you discover to my Soul, the palm of victory, the triumph of Faith, and the sweet footsteps of my Redeemer, leading directly to his Kingdom" (*EBS*, 308).

Elizabeth's encounters with the cross began early in her life. By nature she was not inclined to discuss her problems with others but preferred the solitude of her journal to express her feelings and a period of prayer to commune with God. "I cannot remember ever having expressed Suffering when I have the choice of Silence, and I have indeed been a sufferer, partly from the strong impressions of the mind which I could not efface, and also from causes sufficiently real" (*EBS*, 129).

Embracing the cross like Elizabeth requires an understanding of its role in our life. It is not necessary to be in a particular physical place to encounter the cross but to be receptive to meeting our God in daily life. "We need not go to church to make this communion of suffering, our Savior comes to find us where ever we may be" (*CC*, 54).

Elizabeth dealt with her desire for God along her path in life which was a rough road of the cross. She not only chose this way but cherished its mystery. "Alone on a rock this afternoon, surrounded by the most beautiful scenery, adoring and praising Him for His magnificence and glory, the heavy eye could find no delight. The soul cried out, 'O God! Give Yourself. What is all the rest?' A silent voice of love answered '*I am yours.*' Then, dearest Lord, keep me as I am while I live; for this is true content—to hope for nothing, to desire nothing, to expect nothing, to fear nothing. Death! Eternity! How small are all objects of best, striving, restless, blind, mistaken beings, when at the foot of the cross these two prospects are viewed" (*MS*, 271).

REFLECTION QUESTIONS

Is living the Paschal Mystery central to my life of faith? How do I respond to the crosses in my life? Do I welcome them? What aspects of new life have crosses and suffering brought me? Do I have a sacred place to write about my pain and anger? What cross am I carrying now? Have I told God about it? When the cross becomes too heavy for me, how do I respond? How can I drag it, but not drop it? Am I a cross to anyone else? If so, why and how? Do I help people to carry their crosses? In the spirit of Elizabeth, how do I want to respond to the crosses in my life?

DAY TWELVE

Living the Beatitudes: "According to the Spirit"

FOCUS POINT

The fulfillment of their baptismal consecration by living the Beatitudes is both a personal choice and a common mission for believers. The Sermon on the Mount outlines the way all the people of God are called to discipleship (see Matthew 5:3–12). The Spirit led Elizabeth in becoming a woman of the Beatitudes as she addressed the concerns of persons oppressed by poverty, illiteracy, illness, and injustice. We are called to do the same.

To live according to the Spirit, is to love according to the Spirit.
To live according to the flesh, is to love according to the flesh.
Love is the life of the soul—as the soul is the life of the body....
To live according to the Spirit is to act, to speak, to think in the
manner the Spirit of God requires of us.... To live then according
to the Spirit is to do what faith, hope, and charity teach—either

in spiritual or temporal things (Notation by Elizabeth Seton in her copy of The Following of Christ, *Back Flyleaf).*

The call of the gospel to live the Beatitudes extends to everyone. The human heart longs for happiness. This drive for the Divine draws men and women to the One who alone can satisfy this longing. The gospel invites all baptized persons to seek and find persons in need and respond to them with compassionate zeal (see *AG*, §20). The same Spirit bestows divine gifts of love in various ways for building the kingdom of God.

Living out the spirituality of the Sermon on the Mount has different expressions depending on the commitments of Christians as a spouse, parent, vowed religious, ordained minister, or unmarried layperson. The inner stirrings of the Holy Spirit deep within the human heart shape the sacred journey of each person. At the center of the path to God is the Good News of Jesus Christ (see John 14:6). In the spirit of the Beatitudes, we, like Elizabeth, are challenged to make choices for sake of the mission of the gospel.

LIVING IN THE SPIRIT

Elizabeth had a natural thirst for works of mercy and justice in the spirit of the Beatitudes. Her compassion for persons in need and her commitment to social justice showed itself as early as 1797 in New York City. At that time Elizabeth and other concerned women formed the Society for the Relief of Poor Widows with Small Children. It not only raised funds to benefit the families in need but also spearheaded education for the children, employment for their mothers, and low-income shelter for needy families. Elizabeth held the office of treasurer for several years, during which she showed her emerging leadership skills and keen eye for organizational details.

Many of Elizabeth's friends and two of her sisters-in-law, Eliza

Seton Maitland and Rebecca Seton, also took an active part in the Widows' Society. Together they supported one another in living a vibrant lay spirituality rooted in the Bible. Through the work of their hands and the compassionate charity of their hearts, they energetically trod the roads less traveled to visit the homes of the poor where they met Christ (see Matthew 25:34–40).

Despite the deterioration of her husband's health and the financial ruin of the family business, about six weeks after the birth of her last child, the amazingly resilient Elizabeth resumed her "occupations and duties" which were her lot in life. She also continued to generously give of herself to her neighbors in need. Her attitude of giving was always "with a thankful heart" and in a spirit of adoration of God, "for the opportunities of doing some small service" for her savior (*SW*, 87). Little did Elizabeth realize that within just a few years, she, too, would be a destitute widow with five young children, ranging in age from sixteen months to eight years.

Regarding one home visit to a poor widow, Elizabeth wrote: "These hands prepared the Blessed table. While my soul, and that of my *Soul's Sister* [Rebecca Seton], united" with the dying woman "in joyful praise for our precious privileges, the purchase of Redeeming Love. The *chosen blessed ministering* servant bids us to the feast, and gives it to the departing soul as its '*Passport* to its House.' To me, [it is] as the Seal of High Covenant, which I trust will not be broken in life nor in death—in time nor in eternity" (*SW*, 87).

The social consciousness of the Widows' Society gave clear witness to the gospel. Sometimes its members were called the "Protestant Sisters of Charity" because their devotedness to reaching out to and serving women and children in need was so similar to the Roman Catholic Daughters of Charity in France (see *MS*, 16). The client population grew rapidly and included many immigrants who flocked for relief. Elizabeth and her colleagues were challenged to care for them so that they would not die for lack of assistance. The needs must have seemed overwhelming to Elizabeth in her days as a New York socialite but her faith drew her into Christian service of her neighbors in need. We are called to do the same.

EDUCATING IN THE SPIRIT

Elizabeth championed the cause of free value-based education and religious formation. She adapted the *Common Rules of the Daughters of Charity* of Vincent de Paul and Louise de Marillac for her community. This rule honored Jesus Christ as the source and model of all charity through corporal and spiritual service to persons who were sick and poor. Furthermore, it recommended that the sisters "honor the Sacred Infancy of Jesus in the young persons...whose hearts they are called upon to form to the love of God, the practice of every virtue, and the knowledge of religion, whilst they sow in their midst the seeds of useful knowledge" (*NC*, 243).

Elizabeth approached her mission of education and charity with a deep faith and willingness to take risks when necessary. She believed that "Almighty God always provides" and it was with a heart ever directed upward that Elizabeth committed her cause to Divine Providence (*EBS*, 415). Elizabeth realized that "order must be the foundation of all the good" she and her Sisters of Charity could hope to accomplish (*NC*, 142). God blessed their courageous faith.

The people of the area looked to the Sisters of Charity who "night and day were devoted" to caring for the sick and instructing the ignorant (*NC*, 140). Elizabeth won the respect of the parents of her pupils whose numbers filled the small classrooms of Saint Joseph's House. She was filled with gratitude to God for the blessing of success in her mission. Elizabeth's most earnest hope was that her Adored would do a great deal of good through the apostolic efforts of the Sisters of Charity (see *NC*, 150).

Elizabeth sent Eliza Craig Sadler the following description of her situation: "You know I am as a Mother encompassed by many children of different dispositions, not all equally amiable or congenial, but bound to love, instruct, and provide for the happiness of all. [I must] give the example of cheerfulness, peace, resignation, and consider individuals more as proceeding from the same origin and tending to the same end, than in the different shades of merit or demerit [of their achievements]" (August 3, 1810).

Sensitive to individual differences among the pupils, Elizabeth knew the pain of childhood loneliness and the resulting turmoil which could play havoc on the emotions of adolescent girls. It was important to Elizabeth that Saint Joseph's be not only a learning environment but also a vibrant faith community. She provided time for prayer and also used the singing of hymns as catechetical tools. She arranged for spiritual retreats before first Communion. Through her apostolate of education Elizabeth taught her pupils a living faith and communicated hope to those to whom she ministered. Like Elizabeth, we are also called to transmit gospel values to others.

FAITH, HOPE, AND CHARITY

Elizabeth focused on truth, justice, and charity when providing value-based education for character formation and faith development. In one of the biweekly instructions she gave the boarders, Elizabeth explained her objectives to them: "Your little mother, my darlings, does not come to teach you how to become good nuns nor Sisters of Charity, but rather I would wish to fit you for that world in which you are destined to live, to teach you how to be good mistresses and mothers of families. Yet, if the dear Master selects one among you to be closer to Him, happy are you. God will teach you Himself" (MS, 235).

God graced Elizabeth for her mission in Saint Joseph's Valley. Divine Providence truly blessed her efforts to teach the truths of faith and to do deeds of justice and charity. Elizabeth often referred to "the dirty grain of mustard seed" that was "planted by God's hand in America," citing the large "number of orphans fed and clothed" through the ministry of the Sisters of Charity (NC, 230).

In her instructions to the older students, Elizabeth was mindful that she was forming them for responsible adulthood so that they would be actively involved in living their Catholic faith as future leaders. Sensitive to populations which were underserved and most vulnerable, Elizabeth reminded her listeners that they had "so many opportunities to love our Jesus in his poor" by being involved in social ministry roles (*MS*, 265). When some of the pupils were consistently late for class, Elizabeth imposed a financial penalty, a fine of a penny for charity. The accumulated sum was administered by a small group of students who determined its charitable purpose. In this way the pupils learned lifelong lessons for personal and social responsibility.

Elizabeth was a woman of mission. She took advantage of teachable moments to impress upon others how the love of God requires deeds of charity and justice. Elizabeth could be proactive when it came to advocacy, appealing to others on behalf of someone in need.

One winter evening when it was exceptionally cold she passed a hovel in the woods as she was returning from Old Saint Mary's Church on the Mountain. The miserable hut was barely habitable but through the door she saw several little hungry children poorly clad for the temperature. Her heart went out to the family. As soon as possible upon returning to Saint Joseph's House Elizabeth, with tears in her eyes, told the girls in the study hall about the family's distress.

She recounted the story with such a depth of compassion that each pupil cheerfully contributed to assist the family. Before nightfall Elizabeth and two sisters brought their contributions to the family and assisted the grateful mother in washing and clothing the children. Upon returning, Elizabeth praised the pupils for their generosity and assured them, "Oh, my children, how sweet will be your repose tonight" (*MS*, 266). By baptism, we, like Elizabeth, are called "to do the right and to love goodness, / and to walk humbly" with our God who has a special concern for persons who are poor and in need (Micah 6:8). Elizabeth is a model whom we can imitate.

REFLECTION QUESTIONS

Am I living the Beatitudes in my daily life? How could I grow in practicing the corporal and spiritual works of mercy? Am I in the habit of turning to God throughout the day? If not, what sacred symbol would remind me to direct my heart upwards? When I turn frequently to God within, do I find myself more attentive to my neighbor in need? Who is my neighbor? How would I describe my relationship with God today? Would I like it to be different? How? What can I do about it? In the spirit of Elizabeth, what can I do today to help someone in need?

DAY THIRTEEN

Longing for Eternity: "There Is a Heaven"

FOCUS POINT

In wishing to die in God's grace and friendship, Christians long for eternity. They are called to follow Jesus Christ in imitation of his life on earth. Those who do so will be united to Jesus at death and their entrance into everlasting life will bring them face to face before God. Such was Elizabeth's goal. Her ardent desire for her "dear eternity" made everything else fade into oblivion like the drifting of clouds carried by swift currents of wind.

O my Soul, there is a Heaven! There is a Savior! There is a pure and perfect felicity under the shadow of his wings. There is rest from our labors, peace from our enemies, freedom from our Sins. There we shall be always joyful—always beholding the presence of Him, who has purchased and prepared for us this unutterable glory. "Let not your hearts be troubled. Believe in God; believe also in Me" (Elizabeth Seton to Cecilia Seton, November 19, 1802).

———

E lizabeth desired to be united to her loving Creator forever. From her earliest years she hankered for eternity, often searching the sky and its clouds for her deceased mother and little sister (*SW*, 345). From her perspective of habitually looking up to the sky, Elizabeth was fascinated by the concept of "a beautiful heaven" where her soul would go if she lived in union with Jesus Christ on earth. Her deep faith steadfastly guided her there.

Elizabeth understood eternity as a perfect life with the three Persons of the most Holy Trinity. There she would enjoy being in loving communion with God, the Virgin Mary, the angels, and all the blessed. Elizabeth's preparation for death and thirsting for eternity best describes her burning desire "to depart this life and be with Christ" forever (Philippians 1:23). Heaven is the ultimate end and fulfillment of the deepest human desires which alone satisfy the human heart. Through her earthly pilgrimage Elizabeth found her own unique path to her ever-gracious God as she came to fully understand herself as a disciple of Jesus Christ and attained sanctity (see Revelation 2:17).

THERE IS A SAVIOR

Elizabeth deeply desired union with God and longed for it. Elizabeth kept "looking steadfastly upwards" despite her tenuous attempts early in life of sometimes "reaching for things before" first turning to God (*EBS*, 473). Like ourselves, when Elizabeth focused on God alone, she was better able to discern the aura of "happiness" of attractions and determine their value before making choices and decisions. The Spirit inspired her with courage. Following the Seton family motto, "Hazard Yet Forward," she saw herself as "pressing forward to eternity" in her actions. Yet when faced with sorrow and disappointment, she could be peacefully "quiet and resigned in affliction" without bitterness over her sorrows except for sin (*EBS*, 473).

Elizabeth had a genuine concern for the salvation of souls, especially those most dear to her. At times she turned directly to the Spirit of God and appealed for divine assistance. She prayed for those who needed to mend their ways and turn their lives around for one reason or another. Those persons who might be wavering in their faith were also remembered in prayer so that each member of the human family would be brought to "its center of blessedness" in "our Savior and Redeemer" (*SW*, 91).

Elizabeth believed that promoting the heavenly kingdom among souls was the grand object of one's whole life. This colored how she approached every person and each event. Deeply moved for "such multitudes [of people] in spiritual distress and desolation" as she heard about in her day, she exclaimed: "O, what motives for prayer and exertions of EVERY LOVING SOUL!" (*SW*, 339). Zeal for the salvation of souls consumed her. Her goal was to cultivate "the interest of the heavenly and Everlasting Kingdom in the true spirit of Faith and Eternal hopes" whenever possible (*SW*, 339).

In her poem "Servant of Jesus," Elizabeth reveals her heart's profound propensity for eternity. "Place me amidst the angelic chorus high where Martyrs triumph and where Jesus reigns. View, O my God, this sad and tear-worn cheek, this anguish'd heart, that feeble tott'ring frame. These eyes forever fixed on heaven and Thee—When shall I join thy blest?" (*ASJPH* 3:55).

Elizabeth was a woman of the Spirit, who was liberated to love her God amidst human whims. Despite all appearances of burdensome constraints, she drew strength from an inner well of life-giving grace: "Who can bind the Soul which God sets free?" (*EBS*, 446).

Her faith rested in God's wisdom: "With the strong and ardent Faith with which I receive and dwell on this promise, all is well and resting on the mercy of God" (*EBS*, 221). Like Elizabeth, we are called to not only bring God to the world but the needs of the world to God in prayer.

PURE AND PERFECT HAPPINESS

Elizabeth grew in the spiritual life by listening and responding to the Spirit. Her spiritual path was paved with prayer, scriptural reading, and liturgical worship. The conclusion of a reflection she wrote in her copy of *The Following of Christ* reveals Elizabeth's religious ideal: "Let me mount to God by the stairs of humility on which You came down to me. Let me kiss the path of Mount Calvary sprinkled with Your blood since it is that path alone which leads me to You" (*SW*, 339).

The gift of God's merciful love never ceased to amaze Elizabeth. To her it was a miracle of divine grace and wisdom. She relied on its power to bring her safely to eternal salvation through the maze of her life, whether in the city or countryside. Her salvation would be wrought through the tapestry of her life of ministry woven from events and people, some pleasing and others challenging. Her days, like ours, were filled with busyness, distractions, and interruptions. All did not go as she planned or even wished, yet she maintained an attitude of gracious openness for God to work in her life.

Elizabeth succumbed to religious rapture at times, especially when receiving holy Communion—"God and his creature! WE lost in him!"—and referred to the feast of Trinity Sunday as a "feast of sky gazers" (May 21, 1815). Psalms 103 and 104 moved her to tears, preventing speech except in her heart to her Beloved. In a note to Bruté, she referred to other psalms and exclaimed with intense fervor: "Nothing in our state of clouds and veils I can see so plainly as how the saints died of love and joy, since I so wretched and truly miserable can only read word after word of the blessed 84th and 42nd Psalms in unutterable feelings even to our God, through the thousand pressings and overflowing—God—God—God—that the Supreme delight that He is God and to open the mouth and heart wide that He may fill it" (*ASJPH* 12:44).

Elizabeth was truly a woman of grace whose intimacy with God enkindled feelings of closeness to her Beloved: "Experience daily shows that the actions which we perform for discharging the duties of our state, though they seem sometimes very distracting of themselves, bring US NEARER TO GOD than they remove us from him. They augment the desire of his presence. *He* communicates himself to the soul in such a manner by secret and unknown *ways* in the midst of NECESSARY distractions that it is never delayed" (*EBS*, 463).

UNUTTERABLE GLORY

Always mindful of eternity, Elizabeth was keenly aware of the importance of preparing for death. Her life was marked by being ready to meet her Maker. Elizabeth's fondest wish for those most dear to her was that they have a peaceful death and a blessed eternity and know the "*Peace* which God alone can give" (*EBS*, 223). When surrounded by life-threatening illnesses among her children and young companions at Emmitsburg, Elizabeth told Julia Sitgreaves Scott in a letter that she was "sending my rose buds to blow in heaven" (July 20, 1810).

For the dying she prayed, "O support and strengthen your creatures [entering eternity] that they may then meet You with that Peace which passes all understanding" (*SW*, 91). Elizabeth believed that only God could "give assurance and comfort in that hour" (*SW*, 91). She could not imagine that there would be anyone "who would not wish to secure that Peace" because, according to her thinking, certainly "all [persons] must wish" the blessings of eternity (*SW*, 91).

Virtuous living was Elizabeth's choice. Her life view was holistic. Her religious convictions were linked firmly together in the blessed chain of her life. She often simply prayed that her "adored Lord" would increase her faith and "perfect it" with the sole aim of leading her to eternal life (*EBS*, 479). She lived her faith with integrity. In an illustrated reflection entitled "Jesus, My All," Elizabeth succinctly summarized her life goal of union with God. Elizabeth wrote the first verse around a pen sketch of an angel on which is inscribed the words, "I love." A linked chain appears below and to the left of the line "Link by Link" and encircles the word "One" on each line (*ASJPH* 18:67).

Hasten, Hasten happy moment
Time I bid thee fly
Awake me to Eternity
And bid this body Die
Jesus, infinite goodness

Link by Link the Blessed Chain...

- One Body in Christ—He the Head, we the members
- One Spirit diffused through the Holy Spirit in us all
- One Hope—him in Heaven and Eternity.
- One Faith by His Word and His Church
- One Baptism and participation in the sacraments
- One God—our Dear Lord,
- One Father—We His children—He above all through all, and *in all* (*ASJPH* 18:67; see also Ephesians 4:1–6).

Elizabeth did not fear death. The Eucharist drew her like a magnet to eternity and fed her for living the gospel values each day. This is also our way.

REFLECTION QUESTIONS

What will eternity be like for me? Who have I known that looked forward to heaven? Why? What has been my experience of death? How am I preparing for my own? How would I describe myself in this world? A passenger? A pilgrim? A sightseer? A _____? What has been my path to eternity thus far? How would I like it to be different? What are the magnets in my spiritual life which draw me to God? What are some of my fundamental spiritual practices? In the spirit of Elizabeth, do I pray each day for the grace of a happy and peaceful death?

DAY FOURTEEN

Spiritual Leader:
"The Little Mustard Seed"

FOCUS POINT

Spiritual leaders draw strength for leadership from the Eucharist and the vitality of their union with Christ. The way Jesus and the first disciples loved one another provides a model for Christian living based on the new law of love in the gospel (see John 15:9, 12). As both a leader and a disciple, Elizabeth was impelled by the love of Christ for ministry. She drank deeply from her inner wellspring of divine life which overflowed into her mission of charity and justice for the human family.

This is my commandment that you love one another as I have loved you. The charity of our blessed Lord in the course of His ministry had three distinct qualities which should be the model of our conduct. It was gentle, benevolent, and universal. Its gentleness appeared in all things in His exterior manner, in His forbear-

ance, and moderation in all things. For what had He not to endure from...those to whom He taught his divine truths, with what condescension He managed those opposite Spirits, and accommodated Himself to persuade and gain them. How many rebukes and contradictions did He endure without complaining.... He always desired to have them with Him (Elizabeth Seton, Instruction on Charity, 1).

E lizabeth was a dreamer. She also was a woman of principle led by the Spirit. Her mission gave rise to the Charism of Charity in North America. Based on the tradition of Vincent de Paul and Louise de Marillac, the spirit of the Sisters of Charity consisted in giving themselves to God to love our Lord and serve him corporally and spiritually in the person of the poor (see *NC*, 243).

Like the Father sent Christ, Elizabeth sent her Sisters of Charity to serve the sick poor, care for orphans, and educate needy children. Theirs was a mission, not a job. Their commitment was to an evangelical way of life. Their lifestyle was simple. They were mission-minded women willing to dedicate themselves to the work of the gospel, promoting discipleship of Jesus Christ wherever they went (see Matthew 28:19).

UNIVERSAL

For her community Elizabeth adopted the ideals which flow from the spirit with which Jesus opened his public ministry (see Luke 4:18). Her spiritual vision was rooted in the Christocentric mission expressed first by the prophet Isaiah and fulfilled by Jesus Christ as the Evangelizer of the Poor and source and model of all charity (see Isaiah 61:1)

Elizabeth chose the spiral of apostolic spirituality which flowed from Vincent de Paul's contemplation of *this* Christ. In so doing Elizabeth also befriended his collaborator, Louise de Marillac, another wife, mother, and widow. Together Louise and Vincent formed a community of apostolic women dedicated to the service of persons who were sick and poor in seventeenth-century Paris. Central on Elizabeth's spiritual horizon was the virtue of *charity*. She marked the following biblical passage, which reflected her vision of mission: "That Christ may dwell in your hearts through faith; that you, rooted, and grounded in love may have strength to comprehend...what is the breadth and length and height and depth, and to know the love of Christ" (Ephesians 3:17–21).

Elizabeth connected her baptismal consecration with its expression in her vows as a Sister of Charity. In the meditation she wrote when the Sisters made their vows for the first time in 1813 on the feast of Vincent de Paul, she highlighted how the vows sealed their commitment to God for the service of poor persons for one year (see *SV*, 31). They made four annual vows each year on the feast of the Annunciation (March 25)—poverty, chastity, obedience, and service of the poor.

In choosing the Vincentian charism and spirituality as her pathway, Elizabeth enculturated the tradition of Louise and Vincent for the Catholic Church in America. The Vincentian charism was well-suited for the new American democracy which then lacked native vocations and the availability of value-based education for the formation of lay leaders. Elizabeth placed a high value on teaching the faith and forming a new generation for Church ministry because "the harvest is abundant but the laborers are few" (Luke 10:2). The Church needed workers for ministry just as in our day.

Elizabeth's concern about the formation of new vocations to serve the people of God reminds us that we, too, must pray for new vocations to serve the Church. We must not only beg our Lord for them but invite women and men interested in building up the kingdom of God to consider whether the Spirit is inviting them to be priests, religious, or members of a society of apostolic life.

Elizabeth sometimes fought discouragement and found herself wrestling with temptations and trials in her vocation as a

Sister of Charity. Yet her total trust in God prevailed. Christ the Evangelizer of the Poor drew Elizabeth into her mission as foundress and spiritual leader of the Sisters of Charity. Being given to God in community for the service of poor persons defines the Vincentian vocation. This was Elizabeth's way and is the way of those associated with continuing her tradition of charity into the future. How is the Spirit calling me to be respond to God in my life?

GENTLE

The Vincentian virtues of charity, humility, and simplicity are concrete expressions of the charity charism and became a driving force in Elizabeth's life, generating an inner spiral of discernment for apostolic action. Its incarnational focus of seeing the face of Christ in poor persons shaped Elizabeth's approach to evangelization through education, catechetical instruction, and charitable ministry to poor persons.

Charity. Charity is the enduring and greatest virtue which binds all persons together in unity, builds up the Body of Christ for the kingdom, and is thereby mission-oriented (see 1 Corinthians 13:13). The "virtue of charity" is different from a "feeling of love." Charity is the willing and doing of a true good to another for the motive of pleasing God, whereas human feelings are subjective and emotionally based. The very name, Sisters of Charity, which Elizabeth chose for her community, reflects its identity and essential spirit. This virtue binds its members to Jesus Christ, who is the model *par excellence* in carrying out the corporal and spiritual works of mercy.

Humility. Elizabeth understood humility as the basis of other virtues. Learned from Jesus, meek and humble of heart, humility is like a salve which both heals and promotes healthy interpersonal relations. This same attitude enables men and women to accept themselves and others, with all their strengths and weaknesses—and potential for holiness. Humility, rooted in truth, views self and others with gentleness, acknowledging goodness and talents. This virtue sensitizes us to the neighbor and the truths of God written in ourselves and others.

Simplicity. The quality of simplicity manifests the centrality of the gospel message in word and deed. This virtue contrasts sharply with characteristics of contemporary consumer society. Elizabeth had a reverence for the environment and the gifts of creation wherever she was. Evangelical simplicity is a way of living characterized by speaking the truth, acting with integrity, and avoiding all duplicity. As a Sister of Charity, Elizabeth's simple, poor lifestyle excluded luxury and superfluities.

Elizabeth echoed Vincentian teachings in her instructions to the American Sisters of Charity: "Do we indeed give him [God] the true *service of the heart* without which whatever else we give has no Value?" (*SW*, 326). In forming her companions for their charitable apostolate, Elizabeth brought her associates prayerfully to the fountains of grace in the Eucharist, sacred Scripture, and the writings of Louise de Marillac and Vincent de Paul.

Elizabeth and her sisters understood that they had given themselves to God to serve persons who were poor and in need. This echoes one of the familiar conferences Vincent gave to the early Daughters of Charity, whom he instructed (October 22, 1650). This mission, along with community and spirituality, form the tripod of Vincentian servanthood to which Elizabeth added her nuances for her day. Elizabeth's followers in the Vincentian and Setonian tradition are called to do the same.

BENEVOLENT

Elizabeth planted seeds of God deep in the lives of others. She fostered bonds of faith and charity through her many relationships. When giving instructions on charitable relationships, Elizabeth encouraged her listeners to use everyday opportunities for building charity. In one instruction Elizabeth posed several provocative questions which are applicable today. If God were to "say to us, 'Come learn of Me for I am meek and lowly of heart' and at the same time know how much you ought to be so....

Have I been as my blessed Lord? Have I learned to bear the weaknesses of others? They are obliged to bear with mine…. The bad qualities of others should perfect and purify my Charity rather than weaken it…. If I had to live only with angels this mild and gentle conduct would be of no use, as it would not be required" (SW, 325).

Elizabeth's teachings reflect how she listened and responded to the stirring of the Spirit within her soul. Like ourselves, she sometimes struggled with the problems of interpersonal dynamics, difficult relationships, and sandpaper personalities who rub us the wrong way, but these challenges stimulated her spiritual growth as a woman of deep faith.

It was with a grateful heart that Elizabeth explained to Antonio Filicchi that all the "affairs at Saint Joseph's go on with the blessing of God…to sow the little mustard seed" (September 16, 1817; see also Matthew 13:31). Elizabeth's sole desire for the Sisters of Charity was to "extend their usefulness whenever OUR SWEET PROVIDENCE may call" (October 19, 1820).

Words of faith were among the farewell remarks she made to those gathered around her deathbed: "I am thankful, Sisters, for your kindness to be present at this trial. Be children of the Church—Be children of the Church!" (NC, 234).

Elizabeth's quest was toward the Source of Love. She lived a unified life balanced on the pillars of the Vincentian virtues. Benevolent charity drove Elizabeth toward personal growth and integration. As Elizabeth journeyed toward wholeness and holiness, her inner dynamism enabled her to play the melody of her life on the tension of the many competing demands in her situation.

She lived and served others for the sake of the gospel and integrated prayer, presence, and service into her brief but exemplary life. She reflected extraordinary accommodation to changing circumstances. Elizabeth's model of the Vincentian ideal continues to be an effective one for the contemporary world which invites women and men to live the gospel in word and deed in the spirit of Vincent de Paul and Louise de Marillac.

REFLECTION QUESTIONS

When am I a spiritual leader? A disciple? Do I plant mustard seeds to spread the faith? To promote gospel values? How do I live the virtue of charity in my life? Toward God? The neighbor? People in need? How do I stoke the fire of love for Christ in my own heart? Is God inviting me to dedicate my life to a role of ministry in the Church? As a Deacon? Lay Minister? Servant of the poor? Am I being called to consider a religious vocation? To be a priest? Brother? Sister? How do I want to respond? How will I respond? In the spirit of Elizabeth, am I faithful to the Church?

DAY FIFTEEN

The Cathedral of Creation: "Dear Remembrances"

FOCUS POINT

Powerful encounters with God may occur in a cathedral of creation where life and death are so apparent. Deep faith in God's promise guided Elizabeth throughout her life, enabling her to find God amidst nature and within persons, often meeting her Beloved in a verdant chapel of natural beauty. Such encounters with the Divine allowed Elizabeth to befriend her final passage into the heart of the mystery of divine love for all eternity (see 2 Corinthians 5:1).

Dear remembrances—it would be such INGRATITUDE to die without noting them.... At four years of age sitting alone on a step of the door looking at the clouds...I always loved to play and walk alone—admiration of the clouds—delight to gaze at them, always with the look for my Mother and little Kitty in

92

heaven. Delight to sit alone by the water side—wandering hours on the shore humming and gathering shells—every little leaf and flower or animal, insect, shades of clouds, or waving trees, objects of vacant unconnected thoughts of God and heaven (Elizabeth Seton, Dear Remembrances, 1).

T he tomorrows of our life are built on the foundation of today. Listening and responding to the small and great calls of God in our lives are the experiences by which we meet our grace and grow in the Christian life (see *SW*, 303). The solid foundation of Elizabeth's faith in her gracious God enabled her to deal effectively with human fear and anxiety about her future. Her regular use of the sacrament of reconciliation moved her to ponder preparedness for crossing the threshold of eternity.

Elizabeth valued being in right relationship with her God. "Consider what preparation you would try to bring to the Confession which you believed would be the last you would make in this world" (see *DD*, 34). Elizabeth spent time in her latter years reflecting on the stepping stones of her life (*DD*, 34). This review in the context of faith and hope constitutes the moving mosaic of "Dear Remembrances," a memoir of her most cherished experiences (see *SW*, 344).

LOOKING AT THE CLOUDS

Elizabeth met God not only in her companions but also in nature. A basic principle of her life was that "God is so infinitely present to us that He is in every part of our life and being. Nothing can separate us from Him. He is more intimately present to us than we are to ourselves, and whatever we do is done in him..." (*EPG*, 1). From her earliest days Elizabeth marveled at the transient shapes of the clouds and the mysterious realm of the heavens.

Elizabeth experienced personal darkness with its shadows and obscurity. Her faith-filled solution was to "walk in God's presence continually and securely" (*EPG*, 3). She was conscious of seeking her "eternal treasure" and wished to be ever mindful of God's presence, believing that one "does nothing when alone which they would not do in the presence of a friend" like Jesus (*EPG*, 5). Throughout all of her travels Elizabeth was confident in the one she called the "Father of All Beings" because "God sees each one of us as precisely as if we were *alone* in the wide universe" (*EPG*, 5).

Elizabeth knew the waterways of life. Some had been tumultuous like her passages across the Atlantic; some calm like sailing on the Long Island Sound; some full of hope like the trip to Baltimore; some overflowing with the pain of grief like the one which transported her father's body on his barge along Richmond Creek to the graveyard at Saint Andrew's Episcopal Church for burial on Staten Island (see *EBS*, 186). Through all events she was filled with the fire of an all-consuming love of God which brought reassurance. She marveled at the personal relationship she enjoyed with her Beloved.

"What a deep thought, that God himself is the very life of our being, that He dwells in the Soul of each one of us as in his own element" (*EPG*, 5). Elizabeth pondered why men and women carried "this ever active fire within us.... Yet remain cold, and our icy hearts unconscious of God's presence" (*EPG*, 6). In her thinking, it was "sin or the impurities it has contracted in human nature" which covered "this divine fire and opposes its sacred influence" (EPG, 6). Elizabeth found that a lack of attentiveness to gospel values prevented souls from tending to God as the center of their lives.

Like ourselves, Elizabeth was also very aware of her human limits and human weakness and took her concerns prayerfully to God, who was her "friend" and "Father." "Oh my God, *my blindness* has been truly great—to have thought of you so little through my life, tho' living wholly in you.... Yet, I have thought, acted, and spoken...without respect or love for you, or remembrance that the Soul you have given me was formed only for you and has the power of enjoying You every moment of my life" (*EPG*, 7). This same power is available to every believer who, like Elizabeth, longs for the "blessed presence, the path of life...fullness of joy" (*EPG*, 7).

HUMMING AND GATHERING

Shell seeking and beach combing were among the pleasant pastimes of Elizabeth's girlhood. Her adult memories included some outstanding dreams recalled from those days. Intuitive and introspective by nature, Elizabeth made an inner journey which deepened over the years. In her early searching for gifts from the sea little did she realize she would spend much of her adult life searching for the Giver of all good gifts. She was content with the simple discoveries in nature—sunsets, wildflowers, roses, or "woods, rocks, and walks" in her Valley home and on her beloved Mountain (*SW*, 352).

In the midst of life-changing crises, Elizabeth could still look beyond her worries to admire the majesty of "a beautiful sunset and the view of a bright rainbow which was extended immediately over the Bay" and "observe the different shades of the sun on the clover field before the door" (*EBS*, 185). Her profound trust in God enabled Elizabeth to look beyond the present to eternity and hope for her eternal reward. Total reliance on God was her hallmark even in dark moments, for example, when she "entered the port of Leghorn while the sun was setting" she had "full confidence in God" (*SW*, 347).

After resting or sleeping Elizabeth sometimes recorded her dreams. Often these were full of rich symbols. After the Setons spent their last night at sea before arriving at the port of Leghorn, Elizabeth wrote that in her dream she felt greatly comforted because she "was in the middle Isle of Trinity Church singing with all my soul the hymns at our dear Sacrament" (*EBS*, 251). Her satisfaction in the dream was suddenly shattered by reality when it was explained that the *Shepherdess* "was the first to bring the news of yellow fever in New York" and lacked the required "Bill of Health" for entry (*EBS*, 251). From then on what the Setons encountered seemed like a month-long nightmare.

Among the most touching gifts the Spirit gave Elizabeth during the ordeal of their quarantine was an intuitive reassurance of her husband's salvation. "The night before his death praying earnestly for him that his pardon might be sealed in Heaven and his transgressions blotted out, after praying I continued on my knees and leaned my head on the chair by which I knelt and insensibly lost myself. I saw in my slumber a little angel with a pen in one hand and a sheet of pure white paper in the other. He looked at me, holding out the paper, and wrote in large letters JESUS. This tho' a vision of sleep was a great comfort, and he [William Magee] was very much affected when I told him and said a few hours before he died 'the angel wrote JESUS—he has opened the door of eternal life for me and will cover me with his righteousness'" (*EBS*, 265). What a consoling grace for Elizabeth!

Later in life Elizabeth recalled a "dream in the bay of Gibraltar of the angel on the green hill waiting for me over the black steep mountains" (*SW*, 347). Indeed she had faced mountains of challenges and walked through such darkness since she had that dream in Italy. It was through such "*simple* remembrance" as dreams or the beauty of creation that Elizabeth drew close to her God, who was a "dear friend, a tender Father whose eye" was on her (*EPG*, 8).

WANDERING HOURS

A kaleidoscope of Elizabeth's spirituality contains changing configurations of the wonderful ways the Spirit engaged her heart at different stages of her life. Recalling God's presence was for her "a loving remembrance, not by any particular act of the love of God, but by a secret desire to please" God which was "in itself a mark" of her "love and wish to serve" God alone (*EPG*, 8).

Elizabeth advised her companions to welcome the presence of God within themselves and to become accustomed to a "simple look of the heart to God" which would draw and unite them to the Almighty "in a sentiment of peace and confidence" (*EPG*, 9). Elizabeth instructed her companions that "the Eternal word and the Soul have a language understood by each other...and this takes place in a single moment by the exercise of that *silence* before the Divine Majesty" (*EPG*, 9).

Above all, Elizabeth lived a spirituality focused on the "glory of God and the Salvation" of her soul (*EPG*, 30). One of her fundamental practices included making a pure intention before all her actions. Elizabeth offered her whole self, all her deeds, and the events of the entire day to God upon waking. In this way Elizabeth sealed the gift of herself to God at the dawn of each day.

Elizabeth believed in the importance of renewing her self-offering throughout the day. She also placed a high value on striving to live and serve with a pure intention: "Now it is certain that without a *pure intention* in our actions we can never procure any glory to God, or merit of Salvation for ourselves. For without the *intention* an action is but as shell or a shadow, a Body without a soul which can be neither pleasing nor acceptable to God, while on the contrary there is no action so small which may not be made great and precious before God by an upright and *pure intention*" (*EPG*, 30). Like Elizabeth, we are invited to *be* and to *do* all for God alone.

In her meditation for the Sisters of Charity, "On Service of God," Elizabeth used the paradigm of faith, hope, and charity as a prism for reflecting on the mission of the community and the charism of charity (see *SW*, 326). The love of Jesus Christ impelled Elizabeth in all her actions (see 2 Corinthians 5:14). Inclined to living reflectively, Elizabeth often posed probing questions to her companions like the following. "Do we give him [God] the Service of *Faith*?" "Do we serve God in Hope?" She played on the strings of their emotions, asking directly: "Do we indeed give him the true *service of the heart* without which whatever else we give has no Value?" "Do we consecrate ourselves to God as our *All in All*, with the true Service of the heart?" (*SW*, 326).

Fulfilling her vocation and mission was Elizabeth's personal pathway to eternity—and also is ours. Elizabeth leaves the people of God a great legacy. Her years on earth were an ongoing act of faith. Her life as wife, mother, widow, educator, and spiritual leader made her a saint. Her summary of discipleship gives us the model of a real American woman for all ages.

> We are created in the image of God, and we should breathe and act but for his glory. Our destination is heaven, and *there* every thought and design of our mind should be sent. We are *followers of Christ*, and every action of our life should be done in union with him *since* from Him only they can draw either value or merit (*EPG*, 33).

REFLECTION QUESTIONS

Do I find God in a cathedral of creation amidst the beauty of nature? What are the valleys of peace in my life? What have been the healing waters in my life? The stormy seas? The calming lakes? What streams are pathways for new life? How do these waterways reveal redeeming love in my life? How would I describe my discipleship with Jesus now? How would I like it to be different? What am I willing to do to make that become a reality? In the spirit of Elizabeth, what are the "dear remembrances" of my life for which I am most grateful?

Bibliography

ARCHIVAL SOURCES

AMSV N/P 110: M. II. 12, Elizabeth Bayley Seton, *Leghorn Journal and Diary of 1803–1804* (Unpublished), 16–18.

ASJPH 1-3-3-18:67, Elizabeth Bayley Seton, *Jesus My All* (Unpublished, n.d.).

ASJPH 1-3-3-20C, Elizabeth Bayley Seton, *First Communion Instructions* (Unpublished, n.d.).

ASJPH 1-3-3-3:38, Elizabeth Bayley Seton, *Instruction on Charity* (Unpublished, n.d.).

ASJPH 1-3-3-20D (44–48), Elizabeth Bayley Seton, *Meditations*, "Communion. Preparation, Reception, Thanks, Eternity" (Unpublished, n.d.).

ASJPH 1-3-3-23B (52–61), Elizabeth Bayley Seton, *Meditations*, "Communion of the Cross" (Unpublished, n.d.).

ASJPH 1-3-3-23-B-1 (34–39), Elizabeth Bayley Seton, *Meditations*, "Death in Desire" (Unpublished, n.d.).

ASJPH 1-3-3-20D-2 (103), Elizabeth Bayley Seton, *Meditations, On Still Reading His Prophet and Seeking for Our Only Joy* (Unpublished, n.d.).

ASJPH 1-3-3-25B (19–20), Elizabeth Bayley Seton, *Mother's Advices to Her Daughter, Catherine Josephine Seton* (Unpublished, n.d.).

ASJPH 1-3-3-23B (1–33), Elizabeth Bayley Seton, *On the Exercise of the Presence of God* (Unpublished, n.d.).

ASJPH 1-3-3-23A (17–19), Elizabeth Bayley Seton, *On the Word of God* (Unpublished, n.d.).

ASJPH 1-3-3-3:55, Elizabeth Bayley Seton, *Servant of Jesus* (Unpublished, n.d.).

ASCSH, Elizabeth Seton's copy of *The Following of Christ*, trans. Rt. Reverend Richard Challoner (Mathew Carey: Philadelphia, 1800).

PUBLISHED SOURCES

Walter M. Abbott, S.J., ed., *The Documents of Vatican II* (Herder and Herder: New York, 1966).

Regina Bechtle, S.C., and Judith Metz, S.C., eds., Ellin M. Kelly, mss. ed., *Elizabeth Bayley Seton Collected Writings* (New City Press: New York, 2000).

Saint Francis de Sales, #40 "Instructions for Widows," *Introduction to the Devout Life*, trans. John K. Ryan (Doubleday Image Books: New York, 1972).

Joseph I. Dirvin, C.M., *The Soul of Elizabeth Seton. A Spiritual Portrait* (Ignatius Press: San Francisco, 1990).

Ellin M. Kelly, *Elizabeth Seton's Two Bibles: Her Notes and Markings* (Our Sunday Visitor: Huntington, Indiana, 1977).

Ellin M. Kelly, *Numerous Choirs: A Chronicle of Elizabeth Bayley Seton and Her Spiritual Daughters, Volume I, The Seton Years: 1774–1821* (Daughters of Charity, Mater Dei Provincialate: Evansville, Indiana, 1981).

Ellin M. Kelly, and Annabelle M. Melville, eds., *Elizabeth Seton Selected Writings* (Paulist Press: Mahwah, New Jersey, 1987).

Annabelle M. Melville, *Elizabeth Bayley Seton, 1774–1821* (Charles Scribner's Sons: New York, 1951).

Charles Ignatius White, *The Life of Mrs. Eliza A. Seton* (Edward Dunigan & Brother: New York, 1853).

Charles I. White, *Mother Seton: Mother of Many Daughters*, revised and edited by the Sisters of Charity of Mount Saint Vincent-on-the-Hudson, New York (Doubleday & Company: Garden City, New York, 1949).